Three Australian
feature film
scripts

Published by: IngramSpark Australia (2020)

Other work by Peter Levy:
System error: the diary of my reconfiguration (2018)
Betsy Collins (2019)
Knowing touch (2020)
Three Australian Plays (2020)

Author's Note
I would especially like to acknowledge and thank Sharon Hurst for the cover design and layout.
I would also like to show my gratitude to the office of IngramSpark Australia. Helpful to the enth degree and always available to chat through every crisis, no matter how small or trivial.
Thanks also to Alex Nutman (a.e.nutman@gmail.com) for preparing the files for upload.

61 403 604 213

peter@peterlevy.com.au

ISBN: 978-0-6489459-1-8

Three Australian feature film scripts

Contents

A WAY TO LIVE

<table>
<tr><td>**1.**</td><td>**INT. PAUL'S OFFICE**</td><td>**DAYTIME**</td></tr>
</table>

Paul Lewis has slightly greying hair in his mid-fifties, smart casual dress for a middle class member of the workforce, and of average height. Paul is in an office where he is the centre of attention as he effectively lays out a magazine article much to the applause of his fellow employees.

PAUL

(modestly)

I think that should work now.

FELLOW WORKER

I knew you could fix it

The worker pats Paul on the shoulder. Hymie, the boss, is also watching from a distance and then walks away with a self-satisfied smirk on his face.

Hymie is a weasel of a man, thin and tall with squinty eyes, dark hair, dressed in a dark blue suit.

Paul continues to work on other projects as other workers mill round and congratulate him.

<table>
<tr><td>**2.**</td><td>**INT/EXT. PAUL'S CAR**</td><td>**MID AFTERNOON**</td></tr>
</table>

Paul is driving through the city. His mobile phone rings.

PAUL

Yehlow!

Hymie

(out of shot)

Paul! It's Hymie!

PAUL

What's up?

HYMIE

(out of shot)

What's up you say! I need you here to finish the proofs before we go to press! That's what's up!

PAUL

I'm not too well today, Hymie. I've just been to the doctor and now I'm heading home

(out of shot)

Listen! Just drop by first and do the proofs, OK?

PAUL

Hymie! I'm crook! It'll Really have to wait till tomorrow.

HYMIE
(out of shot)
Don't do this to me Paul! How can I get that raise happening when you pull stunts like this?

PAUL
(annoyed)
Are you for real?

HYMIE
(out of shot)
You bet ya! Hear me! I need you!

Paul gazes out the window as there is a traffic holdup.

HYMIE (cont'd)
(out of shot)
Are you still there?

PAUL
Yeah I'm here!

HYMIE
(out of shot)
Well?

PAUL
I won't be there! I'm going home.

HYMIE
(out of shot)
You're putting me in an awkward spot here Paul. The job comes first! You know that!

PAUL
Well then, I quit! Get some other sucker to lick your boots! Got to go! See you later!

Paul quickly hangs up the phone.
The phone rings again and Paul sees Hymie's name flash up on the screen. With a smile, Paul clicks the phone to the answering machine.

PAUL (cont'd)
(to himself)
Geez! That felt good!

The mobile phone rings again and Paul tenses up as he answers it

PAUL (cont'd)
Hi Shaz?

SHARYN
(out of shot)
How are you, more likely?

PAUL

I'm on my way home, I'll talk to you then, Ok?

SHARYN

(out of shot)

I'll put the kettle on. Oh, Hymie was looking for you, better give him a call.

PAUL

See you soon.

The traffic starts to move and Paul turns the radio on as he drives.

The phone rings again and Paul ignores it.

3.	**EXT. PAUL'S DRIVEWAY**	**LATER**

Paul swings his car into the driveway of his home, turns the engine off and stares out at his house.

Very middle class Tudor style home with a manicured lawn and lovely blooming roses as a centre piece. Other homes in the street are of a similar socioeconomic status.

After a minute, Paul gets out of the car and walks up to his front door.

A neighbour's dog is barking at the wind.

Paul stops in his tracks and goes over to the yapping dog and gives it a good kick!

The dog yelps away.

PAUL

(to the dog)

Disturb my sleep again buster and there'll be more!

Paul goes back to his house and inside the front door.

4.	**INT. INSIDE PAUL'S HOME**	**MOMENTS LATER**

Sharyn is in her late forties, dark hair, and solid build, elegantly dressed.

SHARYN

(concerned)

So what did Brian have to say?

PAUL

(tense)

You know doctors.

SHARYN

(now tense as well)

Oh no!

PAUL

(holding back the tears)

He's given me six months.

*Sharyn clutches hold of Paul. There is an uncomfortable
silence as the words sink in.*

SHARYN
He's not the only doctor around.

PAUL
As he's a friend, he asked me if I'd mind that he share my info with a group
of specialists that he knows.

SHARYN
(teary eyed)
Not even Chemo?

PAUL
They all concluded in my case it wasn't worth going down that track.

SHARYN
What are we going to do?

*Paul struggles to free himself from Sharyn's tight bear-
hug, so that he can breathe.*

PAUL
(with a wry smile on his face)
Jesus! You nearly killed me!

SHARYN
Don't say that! Don't ever say that!

PAUL
I'm sorry! There's no cure and my plan is to go on as if I'm OK. It's not
going to change anything but I need some time without any pity attached
to everything I do.

SHARYN
(a little shocked)
Not even the kids?

PAUL
Especially not them! I don't want their last memories of me to be filled
with sympathy. Anyway they are away living their own lives.

SHARYN
Oh god! Are you going to continue working?

PAUL
No! I told Hymie that I quit!

SHARYN
Wow!

PAUL
He pushed me and I, I …

SHARYN
Pushed him back?

PAUL

I can't do this without your total support, and I know this will be hard on you.

SHARYN

This is going to be a nightmare, but I'll try! What are we going to tell our friends?

PAUL

Actually I don't want to tell anyone. Maybe Andy and Rita.

SHARYN

You can just tell everyone you've retired!

---

5.   INT. BEDROOM   EVENING

Paul and Sharyn are madly making love.

Paul is asleep and snoring loudly while Sharyn is sobbing uncontrollably into her pillow.

The neighbour's barking dog is also heard.

In a dream sequence, Paul is seen taking out a hand gun and shooting the dog, and being very happy about it. The neighbour comes over angrily and Paul shoots him too.

---

6.   INT. BEDROOM   MORNING

Paul wakes up first and gazes fondly at Sharyn who instinctively opens her eyes.

They kiss.

PAUL

How did you sleep, babe?

SHARYN

Well, if you must know, badly. It took me forever to nod off, I was so upset.

PAUL

Sorry about that.

SHARYN

And that bloody dog didn't help as well!

PAUL

I'll talk to Matt about his dog ... we'll get through this.

SHARYN

I know. I have to come to terms with the magnitude of it, is all.

Together, Paul and Sharyn bundle into the bathroom and the sound of the shower is soon heard.

---

7.   INT. KITCHEN AREA   LATER

They are finishing off their eggs on toast and about to start in on their coffees.

PAUL

I'd like to go down to the bayside and get some top notch fishing gear for you and me.

SHARYN

I see.

PAUL

It's something I used to talk about doing, but never did. You don't mind do you?

SHARYN

How can I refuse you at a time like this.

PAUL

You'll love it! Just give it a go and see how you feel.

SHARYN

Is that how you see the rest of your life?

She suddenly realizes the weight of her words.

SHARYN (cont'd)

Oh! I'm sorry babe! We can give it a try, if you like!

---

8.   **INT. BAYSIDE FISHING STORE**   **MORNING**

The owner of the store is explaining the different rods and reels.

SHOP OWNER

Around here you are only going to require basic gear for the smaller fish, as we don't really cater for the biggens anymore.

PAUL

No big fish around here?

SHOP OWNER

Totally fished out for the past two years.

SHARYN

What sort of fish can we catch then?

SHOP OWNER

Oh, the whiting, some salmon, a few gar fish. Oh yeah, plenty of blowies!

The shop owner lets out a hearty laugh.

PAUL

What sort of bait do you recommend?

SHOP OWNER

A packet of the good old frozen squid should do the trick.

PAUL

Ok we'll have the rods and reels, a packet of that bait and if you could chuck in a few odds and ends like extra sinkers and spinners, we'll be done.

SHOP OWNER

Too easy!

The shop owner gathers all the goods together and writes down the list on a sheet of paper, tallying the amount on a calculator.

PAUL

What's the damage?

SHOP OWNER

Two hundred and fifty six dollars and twenty five cents! Two hundred and fifty will do.

PAUL

(Paul hands over his credit card)
Thanks mate!

---

9.   EXT. THE FISHING PIER   **MOMENTS LATER**

About six older fishermen are on the pier and they all look up and acknowledge Paul and Sharyn as the pair find a spot to lay down all their tackle.

Paul starts putting the rods together and fitting the reels.

PAUL

Could you pass me that screwdriver please babe?

SHARYN

This one?

PAUL

That's the one! Thanks!

After about an hour of fiddling, both rods are ready and Paul baits them and casts one as far off as he could. Doing the same for the other rod, he hands Sharyn a rod.

SHARYN

What am I supposed to do now?

PAUL

We're going to catch some fish, just you wait and see.

Paul suddenly notices that there is only one of the old men left on the pier, and he is packing up his gear.

PAUL (cont'd)
(to the fisherman)
How come everyone's leaving?

Fisherman
(heavy accent)
Too late now for the fishies mate. We come back tomorrow.

PAUL

What time do you guys get here?

FISHERMAN

Oh around four O'clock, is good time.

PAUL

Thanks, see you later!

The fisherman waves and smiles as he leaves the pier.

SHARYN

Four O'clock! Are you kidding me?

PAUL

It'll be alright. You'll see!

An hour passes and Paul and Sharyn pack up and head off.

10.	**INT. BEDROOM**	**NIGHT TIME**

The barking dog is heard again.
Paul gets up into his dressing gown and starts to make for the door.
Sharyn stirs.

SHARYN

(in a whisper)

That dog again?

PAUL

I know what to do.

Sharyn goes back to sleep as Paul goes outside.

11.	**EXT. PAUL'S CAR**	**NIGHT**

Paul is seen driving across the Westgate Bridge with a dog sitting next to him barking at the cars he can see through the window.

Paul parks in a quiet street near a park, gets out and beckons for the dog to do the same.

The dog bounds out and appears very happy for the attention.

Paul quickly jumps back in the car and speeds off leaving the dog stranded.

PAUL

(gleefully to himself)

How easy was that!

12.	**INT. BEDROOM**	**MORNING**

The alarm goes off and startles the now wakened Paul and Sharyn.

SHARYN

Paul! It's still night-time!

                              PAUL
                            (excited)
                     I know! It's three thirty!

                            SHARYN
                      You go if you want to!

                              PAUL
                          Oh, come on!

                            SHARYN
            I'll have breakfast with you when you get back. OK?

Paul smiles tenderly at Sharyn and kisses her as she falls back into a slumber.

Paul slides out of bed and grabs some clothes as he goes.

---

13.   INT. KITCHEN AREA   MOMENTS LATER

Paul dresses and grabs an apple from the fridge as he leaves the house.

---

14.   INT. THE FISHING PIER   LATER

The same men are already there, and there is a silent acknowledgement of Paul as he baits up and throws a line in.

The old men occasionally speak Greek between themselves.

Suddenly Paul gets a tug on his line and excitedly he starts winding in a medium size fish.

                              PAUL
                       You little beauty!

One of the other fishermen, Chris, looks over to Paul.

Chris is tall and dark haired, dressed in old jeans and a windjammer, and wears a beanie on his head, a weathered face and moustache.

                            CHRIS
                       Slowly, slowly!

                            PAUL
                         Ok! Thanks!

Chris gets a net on a pole and gently scoops the fish into it.

                            CHRIS
                       There you go!

                            PAUL
                     Efcharisto poli!

                            CHRIS
                          (laughing)
                       Are you Greek?

                              PAUL
                          (also laughing)
                            Not yet!

*Paul unhooks the fish and looks around as to where to put
it. Chris smiles and points to his bucket.*

                              CHRIS
            Put it in here! You can take it when you leave.

                              PAUL
                           Thanks again!

Paul baits up and casts off again.
Pretty soon the other fishermen are pulling in fish as well.

                              CHRIS
                     Too early for your wife?

                              PAUL
              You got it in one! She'll be surprised all right.

*After a frenzy of catching for about a half hour, it all dies
down to a peaceful silence .*
*Paul nods to Chris and makes his way back to his car with
a couple of fish in hand.*

---

15.   INT. KITCHEN AREA   **LATER**

*Paul is cooking some fish in a pan when Sharyn comes
down in a dressing gown. She kisses Paul on the lips.*

                             SHARYN
                           How was it?

                              PAUL
                           (beaming)
                 It was great! Nice guys as well.

                             SHARYN
                            Oh yeah?

                              PAUL
The Greeks are fun! I'm sorry I didn't learn more phrases to amuse them
                             with.

*Sharyn gets some plates from a cupboard as Paul serves
up the fish.*

                         PAUL (cont'd)
                 Can't get any fresher than that?

                             SHARYN
        I guess not. What are your plans for the rest of the day?

PAUL

I'm not sure. I thought we might take a drive somewhere. Have you got anything on?

SHARYN

I was supposed to meet up with Jo for a coffee around eleven. I could cancel it!

PAUL

No, you do it, I'll take a nap and maybe we'll do something late afternoon.

SHARYN

If you don't mind?

PAUL

Of course not! Don't go silly around me.

SHARYN

(a little teary)
I'll try not to.

PAUL

Good girl!

Another morning in the bedroom of Paul & Sharyn
Half asleep Sharyn beckons to Paul.

SHARYN

Yesterday I forgot to mention the leak in the shower

PAUL

Shit! That's not good! Get a tradesman in.

SHARYN

Why don't you just clean the leaves from the gutter? It won't kill you!

Paul looks blankly at Sharyn, who has now lapsed back into sleep. Paul leaves the house.

16. EXT. THE FISHING PIER	**MORNING**

Paul wanders down to his usual spot and sees Chris fishing
alone on the pier.

PAUL

Kalimera!

CHRIS

(looking up with a smile)
Kalimera!

Paul baits up and throws his line in.

PAUL

Where is everyone?

CHRIS

Church today for the Orthodox.

PAUL

Not you?

CHRIS

Not me!

The men settle into their fishing, but nothing is biting.

PAUL

(laughing)

I think the fish have gone to church as well today.

CHRIS

It's the wind, this morning. No good for pier fishing.

PAUL

Oh! I didn't know!

CHRIS

Maybe we could share a little boat and go a few metres out?

PAUL

(nodding)

Why not.

---

17. **EXT. THE OPEN SEA**   **MOMENTS LATER**

After a few minutes the outboard motor of the little dinghy is switched off and Chris has thrown an anchor over the side.

CHRIS

Now we really fish!

Both men bait up and cast off.
Pretty soon Paul is getting a tug on his line.

PAUL

(excitedly)

I've got one!

CHRIS

Didn't I tell you?

Some decent sized fish are caught in a frenzied half hour and Chris starts to clean them with his knife.

PAUL

Sharyn will be surprised, I'll bet!

Chris looks up from what he is doing and faces Paul, the knife still in his hand, dripping with fish blood.

CHRIS

So what do you do for a living?

PAUL
I'm just marking time.

CHRIS
I thought there was something, but I couldn't put my finger on it.

PAUL
What about you?

CHRIS
(smiling)
Fucking army, fucking prison!

PAUL
What happened?

CHRIS
You really want to know?

PAUL
If you want to tell me.

Chris puts the knife down and sits opposite Paul.

CHRIS
I was a sniper on the Albanian border.

PAUL
Really?

CHRIS
Three years later, I was recruited by another army.

Chris smiles gingerly at Paul, studying him with his eyes.

CHRIS (cont'd)
Sort of like the Sicilian mafia.

PAUL
Is this the truth?

CHRIS
Oh yes! Friends from my army days recommended me to the Don and he sent for me.

PAUL
Wow!

CHRIS
All I had to do, was the occasional hit, when asked. I actually looked forward to the requests.

PAUL
How many requests did you do?

CHRIS
Over a twelve year period, I would say I killed around four persons a year.

PAUL
You mean fifty men?

CHRIS
(chuckling)
Not all were men!

PAUL
What!

CHRIS
I remember three women.

PAUL
Jesus!

Chris goes back to cleaning the fish as if nothing important had been said.

Paul stares at him in disbelief.

PAUL (cont'd)
You said something about prison. What was that all about?

CHRIS
My last job did not go according to my plan. I was setup by my Don who figured I was a liability.

The two men stare intensely at each other.

CHRIS (cont'd)
The bloody judge gave me twenty five years without parole.

PAUL
Shit!

CHRIS
I was hoping he would execute me, but, as you can see, I survived.

PAUL
What happened to the Don?

CHRIS
Died of old age. I emigrated here where my sister lives, and I fish.

PAUL
That is some story. I've always admired people who were fearless in standing up to anyone. Not like me!

CHRIS
It takes all kinds to make up the world.

PAUL
(laughing)
My very words!

CHRIS
Pass me that bag over there please.

PAUL
Sure!

Chris starts to put the cleaned fish in the bag and throws the remains over the side.

CHRIS
Fish got to eat too!

Chris puts the engine back on as Paul hauls the anchor back into the boat.

They are soon chugging back to the pier.

18.	**EXT. THE FISHING PIER**	LATER

Chris and Paul climb out of the boat, tie it up and share out the fish.

CHRIS
You take this lot, and I'll have the rest. Fair enough?

PAUL
You bet! See you later!

Paul heads off to his car.

19.	**EXT. PAUL'S DRIVEWAY**	

It's late afternoon and Paul is checking his car for rust patches.
Matt, about fifty, heavy set, brute type, neighbour to Paul comes over to chat.

MATT
Hi Paul! Car trouble?

PAUL
(looking up a bit surprised)
Rust!

MATT
You haven't seen my dog have you?

PAUL
(casually)
No! Run off has he?

MATT
Not sure! Give me a call if you do.

PAUL
Sure!

Paul goes back to his car work and Matt slinks back across his border line.
Paul has a wry smile starting to appear on his face.

<table><tr><td>**20.**</td><td>**EXT. THE FISHING PIER**</td><td>**MORNING**</td></tr></table>

Paul is sitting next to Chris on the pier. The other fishermen are also there.

<table><tr><td>**21.**</td><td>**EXT. THE FISHING PIER**</td><td>**ANOTHER MORNING**</td></tr></table>

Paul carries his gear over to where Chris is sitting and sits next to him.

The other fishermen acknowledge Paul with a smile.

CHRIS
There's some good ones this morning.

PAUL
I won't mind that, one little bit.

Pretty soon all the men are catching fish.

PAUL (cont'd)
(to Chris)
Why don't you come back to my house for breakfast this morning?

CHRIS
(looking at Paul very seriously)
I don't think so.

PAUL
Come on! It would really mean a lot to me!

Both men stare at each other for quite some time. Paul shrugs his shoulders and opens his arms in an inviting gesture.
Chris laughs out loud.

CHRIS
(quietly to Paul)
Ok! Just this once! Alright?

Chris and Paul wait till the other fishermen head off and then walk to the parking lot to their cars.

<table><tr><td>**22.**</td><td>**EXT. PIER PARKING LOT**</td><td>**MOMENTS LATER**</td></tr></table>

Paul points out his car.

PAUL
That's mine over there. Just follow, I'll drive slowly.

The cars pull out into the morning traffic.
Chris is driving an old Ford station wagon with paint and rust starting to appear on the trim.

<table><tr><td>**23.**</td><td>**EXT. KITCHEN AREA**</td><td>**LATER**</td></tr></table>

Paul is cooking up some fish and the coffee machine is

buzzing away. Chris is sitting at the kitchen table reading a newspaper.

Sharyn comes in wearing a very sheer negligee and is somewhat surprised to see Chris at the table. She rushes out of the room.

PAUL
(calling out to Sharyn)
Sorry hon! I thought you'd appreciate not being woken up!

SHARYN
(pissed off but controlled)
You could have rung me!

PAUL
I will next time! Do you want some brekkie?

SHARYN
Ok! I'll be there in a minute!

Paul smiles awkwardly at Chris.

Sharyn comes back in a dressing gown, buttoned to the top, and smiles at Chris.

PAUL
Sharyn, this is Chris, one of my fishing buddies.

SHARYN
Oh yes, I do remember seeing you on the pier. How are you?

CHRIS
I'm Ok thank you. I'm sorry if I caused you any trouble.

SHARYN
(looking at Paul)
Oh that's all right! **You** didn't do anything!

Paul serves up the fish and the coffee and they all dig into it.

CHRIS
Mmm! Nice coffee alright! I prefer the Greek, but this is very nice.

SHARYN
What part of Greece are you from?

CHRIS
A little village on the mainland, near Thessaloniki.

SHARYN
I've never been that far north.

PAUL
Didn't you go to Volos a few years ago? That's north!

                                    SHARYN
                            Oh yes! Volos, do you know it?

                                    CHRIS
                  Of course! It's a big town. I've spent a lot of time there.

Chris winks at Paul and smiles.

                                CHRIS (cont'd)
                            Twenty five years to be exact.

                                    PAUL
                                More fish anyone?

                                    SHARYN
                                  Not for me!

                                    CHRIS
                                   (getting up)
               I've had enough too, thanks! I should be getting home as well. My fish
                                  need my attention.

                                    SHARYN
                            It was nice to meet you, Chris.

                                    CHRIS
                                    Me too!

Paul walks Chris to the door.

                                CHRIS (cont'd)
               You know, it is the first time anyone has ever invited me to their home.

Chris goes outside and Paul wanders back to the kitchen.

24.   **EXT. THE FISHING PIER**   **MORNING**

*Paul and Chris are cleaning some fish together as the other
Greek fishermen wander off.*

                                    PAUL
                         So how did you get away with it for so long?

                                    CHRIS
                             With what, are you asking?

                                    PAUL
                                Hitting all those people.

                                    CHRIS
                                    Oh that!

                                    PAUL
                                 What was it like?

                                    CHRIS
                I'll tell you. It made me feel alive and dead at the same time.

PAUL
But you were good at it! Weren't you?

CHRIS
(showing Paul a fish)
This one we throw back, ok?

PAUL
Sure!

CHRIS
Why do you want to know these things?

PAUL
I have some unfinished business.

CHRIS
(laughing)
You?

PAUL
Some people have done bad things to me and,

CHRIS
Why now, why not then?

PAUL
I didn't have what it takes.

CHRIS
And now you do?

PAUL
Now I am dying.

Chris looks directly into Paul's eyes.

CHRIS
You think you know me now? You don't know me!

Paul winces a little, but keeps the stare going.

CHRIS (cont'd)
What do you want from me?

PAUL
Advice. I need to do this right, if I'm going to do it at all.

CHRIS
And your wife?

PAUL
She knows nothing about it, and I'd like her never to know!

*There is an awkward silence as the men eye each other
suspiciously.*

PAUL (cont'd)
(nervously)
Haven't you ever needed someone's help?

CHRIS
Of course!

PAUL
I'm asking for your help.

Another silence.

PAUL (cont'd)
I don't want Sharyn involved. This is between you and me. Ok?

CHRIS
Ok with me. Who is this target and where does he live and where does he work?

Paul takes a big gulp and looks up to the sky for a brief second.

PAUL
My ex lawyer, Raymond Willis, lives in The Docklands and has an office on Collins Street.

CHRIS
I never have liked lawyers!

PAUL
He was my friend as well!

CHRIS
Oh! I see! A crime of passion?

PAUL
He betrayed me and did not have the decency to even apologize!

CHRIS
Lawyers!

PAUL
He knew I was the man I was, and he took me for a ride!

Both men stare at each other. Paul has a pleading look.

CHRIS
You have no idea what you're getting yourself in to.

Both men continue to stare at each other.
Paul's eyes are pleading to Chris.
Chris gets a cold look in his eyes and then a little gleam of excitement.

CHRIS (cont'd)
I'll be the teacher. You will be the one who does the deed. Ok?

                              PAUL
                               OK!

*A bead of perspiration forms and drops from Paul's
forehead as both men share a moment of contemplation.*

                             CHRIS
Once you do this thing, there is no coming back from it.

                              PAUL
                    What have I got to lose?

                             CHRIS
                          Your soul?

                              PAUL
                       Don't have one!

*Both men laugh heartily. The other fishermen look
suspiciously at them both, but mainly at Chris.*

                             CHRIS
Ok you come to my place for breakfast this time and we can talk more
                           freely.

*Everyone packs up their gear and Paul & Chris walk off to
their cars.*

Paul is seen on the mobile talking to Sharyn.

25.   INT. CHRIS'S KITCHEN

*A pan is sizzling away and a pot of Greek coffee is gently
puffing out steam.*

                             CHRIS
                 (laughing as he pours the coffee)
                 Now you will have real coffee!

*Paul is very quiet and wide eyed as they have their
breakfast.*

                       CHRIS (cont'd)
I'm thinking that a knife and gun might be a little hard for you. And messy.

                              PAUL
                        What else then?

                             CHRIS
           Poison is one I often used to good effect.

                              PAUL
                           Poison?

                             CHRIS
              Oh yes! Oldest form of killing.

PAUL
How?

CHRIS
You mean how to make it up and how to deliver it . . . without being
caught.

Chris lets out a big laugh.

PAUL
I guess so.

CHRIS
Well, when I was in the Don's army, a fellow soldier gave me a recipe that
was really quite amazing.

PAUL
And?

CHRIS
He called it "Miraios" and it penetrates naked skin leaving very little trace.
Like a heart attack or stroke.

PAUL
Wow! How do you get it to the victim without getting it on yourself?

CHRIS
Many ways! Write a letter with a card covered in it. Not the best way!

PAUL
What do you suggest?

CHRIS
You touch him, of course wearing a protective glove, and then about four
hours later it suddenly kicks in.

PAUL
Miraios!

CHRIS
I can make it for you right here. Maybe it will take me three or four days
to get the ingredients. I always buy things over a period of time to avoid
suspicion.

PAUL
Expensive?

CHRIS
Not really ... common things on their own are pretty harmless ... but mix
the right cocktail and you get Miraios.

Both men stare at each other. Paul's mobile goes off and
he answers it ... Still staring at Chris.

PAUL
Hi babe ... yeh breakfast was nice ... I'll be home in a half hour ... OK, see
you then ... Bye!

                              CHRIS
                        You're a lucky man.

                              PAUL
                            I know.

                              CHRIS
                 You want me to make this up for you?

Paul is deep in thought.

                        CHRIS (cont'd)
                          Are you sure?

Paul snaps out of his daze and smiles.

                              PAUL
                          Let's do it!

Both men return knowing gazes.

26.   INT. PAUL'S HOUSE

Paul comes inside his home and calls out.

                              PAUL
                        Hi babe I'm back!

Sharyn rushes to meet him.

                        PAUL (cont'd)
                          What's up?

                            SHARYN
                  Hymie's here in the kitchen.

Paul marches into the kitchen. Hymie looks up from his coffee.

                            HYMIE
                    You're a hard man to catch.

                              PAUL
                         (somewhat harshly)
                    What are you doing here?

                            HYMIE
      Your old job and the raise you always wanted. Come in tomorrow and …

                              PAUL
                   You just don't get it do you?

                            HYMIE
                          Get what?

                              PAUL
      You could offer me triple the deal … You're a pompous self-righteous old
            fart! Best thing I ever did was leaving you!

HYMIE

Well I...

PAUL

Come here again uninvited and you'll need a dentist! Stand up and leave now!

Hymie being a much bigger man towers over Paul and is in a state of shock.

SHARYN

(smirking)

I guess that means No to the job. I better see you out.

Sharyn escorts Hymie to the door with a wry smile on her face.

PAUL

That felt good!

SHARYN

What's come over you all of a sudden?

They look deeply at each other.

PAUL

Life's too short to waste it on idiots.

SHARYN

What about our other friends?

PAUL

Let's take it as we come to it, eh?

Paul goes up the stairs to the bedroom.

SHARYN

Where's today's catch?

PAUL

Oh shit! I knew there was something I'd forgotten.

---

27.   INT. PAUL'S HOUSE   **LATER THAT NIGHT**

Sharyn & Paul are entertaining their good friends Andy & Rita.

Andy is lean and very tall, full headed dark hair, youthful appearance in his mid-fifties, smart casual dress.

Rita is petit, around fifty, long blond hair, sexy looking outfit, plenty of jewellery on display.

SHARYN

It's nothing special.

RITA

You always say that and put us under such pressure.

SHARYN

(laughs nervously)

That's what friends do.

PAUL

So Andy, how's the new factory coming along?

ANDY

Slow. I'd say another month before we can start producing again.

PAUL

That is slow.

ANDY

And you? How's it all going?

Paul looks over at Sharyn and gives her a smile.

PAUL

Well, to be honest, there are some big changes going on in our lives at the moment …

ANDY

Really?

PAUL

Firstly, and you are the only ones I'm sharing this with, I got a cancer that is inoperable...

RITA

Oh my god!

PAUL

I haven't told the kids yet.

SHARYN

We thought we'd carry on as if nothing had happened for a bit while we can.

Andy goes very pale and seems at a loss for words.

ANDY

Geez … Christ … So what are your immediate plans?

PAUL

Well I quit my job and I'm doing a bit of fishing.

ANDY

If there's anything I can do … You know I'm there.

PAUL

Thanks, it's OK for now … no major expenses, no treatment cost and the house is paid off.

SHARYN

We always planned to retire someday. We have six to nine months to do just that.

PAUL

That's it! I know it's a shock, but let's not spoil the time we have together. There's nothing more we can do about it.

ANDY

I need a drink!

Andy hugs Paul and Rita gives Sharyn a hug. Teary eyes all round.

28. INT. BEDROOM	**NIGHT TIME**

Paul is sound asleep with the occasional snort.

Sharyn is wide awake gently sobbing.

29.   EXT. THE FISHING PIER

Paul wanders down the pier, spots Chris and settles next to him. The other fishermen don't take much notice.

PAUL

Good morning! I slept in. Late night.

CHRIS

Kalimera!

PAUL

Catching any?

Chris points to his half full bucket.

CHRIS

About an hour ago they came jumping out of the water. Now all asleep I think.

PAUL

Lucky you!

Paul baits up and throws a line in.

PAUL (cont'd)

You never know unless you have a line in.

CHRIS

Ha Ha ... I think it's over for today my friend.

PAUL

Maybe.

Chris gives Paul a little smile.

30.   INT. CHRIS'S KITCHEN

Chris puts a coffee on the stove as Paul fishes out a twenty dollar bill and lays it on the table.
Chris places a little bottle on the table.

CHRIS

This will do the job. Be very careful not to get any on you.

PAUL

I will, I will. Thank you.

CHRIS

Have you thought of a plan of action?

PAUL

I thought I would go down to where he lives on The Docklands and watch
him go to his office for a couple of days.

CHRIS

Good idea. Wear a hat or beanie and a pair of dark glasses.

PAUL

Just for looking?

CHRIS

Absolutely! You never know who is looking at you … remember that!

PAUL

OK I will.

Chris serves up the coffee.

CHRIS

And I think I should keep this little bottle until you are ready to do this
thing. I'll come with you on the big day.

PAUL

(looking somewhat relieved)
Tomorrow I'll go down there at seven O'clock and see what happens.

CHRIS

Good. You can report back to me at the end of the week.

---

31.   **INT. A DELI ON THE DOCKLANDS**

*It's an early morning with plenty of office workers rushing
past. Paul is beanied up with dark sunglasses drinking a
coffee. His eyes are glued on the apartment block opposite.*

*Every time anyone comes out of the block, Paul checks his
watch and searches for his target.*

WAITRESS

Another coffee, love?

PAUL

(nervously)
That would be nice. Thanks.

Paul sees the time is nine thirty and gets up and leaves.

32.   **EXT. THE FISHING PIER**

Paul is next to Chris fishing.

PAUL

I've been there twice and he hasn't showed.

CHRIS

(smiling)
You have to be patient ... it's like fishing ... keep trying.

PAUL

I will be there tomorrow. I don't want the deli where I watch from to get suspicious.

CHRIS

Now you're thinking like a killer!

They both look around to see if the other men were listening. They both let out a relieving laugh.

33.   **INT. A DELI ON THE DOCKLANDS**

Paul checks his watch as a new batch leaves the building and, to his shock, sees Raymond Willis striding out with a younger lady.
Raymond is tall, blond hair, well dressed in a suit and long black coat. The lady is wearing a typical secretary's black dress and high heel shoes.

RAYMOND

(smugly)
Just alter the entries in my day book. That'll cover our tracks.

LADY

(amazed)
Can you do that?

RAYMOND

I can do anything!

Paul's phone rings.

PAUL

Hi babe.

SHARYN

(out of shot)
Where are you? I can hear traffic.

PAUL

Trying a new spot down near the city.

SHARYN

(out of shot)
Any luck?

                                    PAUL
                              Just had a bite!

                                  SHARYN
                                (out of shot)
          Don't forget we have a meeting with the accountant at eleven.

                                    PAUL
          Thanks. It did slip my mind. I'll pack up now and see you soon.

                                  SHARYN
                                (out of shot)
                            Sounds good. Love you.

                                    PAUL
                          Love you too. See you soon.

                  Paul looks around the deli and quietly leaves.

34.   INT. A DELI ON THE DOCKLANDS   ANOTHER DAY

                  *Paul is seen sipping a coffee and watching as Raymond
                  Willis again strides out to his office.*

35.   EXT. THE FISHING PIER

                  Paul chatting with Chris.

                                   CHRIS
                          Did you check the exact time?

                                    PAUL
                     Twenty past eight on the dot. Both times!

                                   CHRIS
                              Ok this is good.

                                    PAUL
                                  (excited)
                          It's now or never isn't it?

                                   CHRIS
          I think tomorrow we hire a little boat as before and just do it.

                                    PAUL
                                    Ok.

                                   CHRIS
                  Meet me here at seven thirty and away we go.

36.   EXT. A BOAT ON THE SEA

                  *With Chris at the wheel, Paul is shivering a little with the
                  cold and nerves.*

                                    PAUL
                                 Bloody cold.

CHRIS
The least of our worries.

They exchange looks.
The Docklands' pier looms up in the distance.

CHRIS (cont'd)
There she is. Better put those gloves on now.

PAUL
Ok.

Paul gloves up with skin tight rubber gloves as Chris steers the boat to an empty mooring space.

CHRIS
(looking at his watch)
You've got about fifteen minutes.

Chris pulls the little bottle from his vest and unscrews the lid.

CHRIS (cont'd)

Whatever you do. Don't touch anything or anybody after you've done this thing! Remember to take hold of him with both hands and keep the grip for a few seconds to be sure.
The eye each other nervously.

CHRIS (cont'd)
Come straight back here and I'll take the gloves from you. Ok with all of that?

PAUL
I got it!

CHRIS
Good luck!

PAUL
Yeh.

Paul holds out his hands as Chris pours the liquid onto the gloves. Without a word, Paul neatly, without touching the sides of the pier, hops from the top of the cabin onto the pier and starts walking towards the office block.

---

37.   EXT. OFFICE BLOCK EXTERIOR

Paul waits for five minutes before seeing Raymond Willis leave his building and about to enter the street on his own.
Paul calls out to him with his hand extended.

PAUL
Raymond!

Raymond looks around and is somewhat surprised to see Paul, especially in his outfit.

RAYMOND
Paul?

Paul moves closer to him.

PAUL
How have you been? It's been quite a while!

Raymond takes the extended hand to shake it and Paul clasps his other hand over the top to clamp it in.

RAYMOND
What's with the glove?

PAUL
Fishing by the pier. It's so good to see you. We should get together sometime for a meal!

Raymond is a little shocked by the warm reception and manages to get his hand back with a little effort.

RAYMOND
I'll call you when I have my diary.

PAUL
You do that!

Raymond strides out with a handkerchief in hand trying to wipe off the stickiness and Paul leans up against the office building with perspiration coming down his face.

Paul goes to wipe the sweat off. Suddenly remembers his gloves. Curses to himself and scurries off back to the boat.

---

38.   EXT. BACK ON THE BOAT

Chris quietly takes Paul's gloves off and then his own. He places them in a garbage bag and seals the top of it.

CHRIS
So, how did it go?

PAUL
Let's get out of here. It went like clockwork!

Chris starts the engine and they motor off.

---

39.   INT. PAUL'S KITCHEN AREA

Paul is having a cup of coffee as Sharyn comes down to join him.

SHARYN
Hi babe. How did it go today?

PAUL

No fish, but a lot of fun.

SHARYN

I don't know what you see in it.

The phone rings and Sharyn answers it.

SHARYN (cont'd)

Hello, Sharyn here.

We hear some muffled sounds

SHARYN (cont'd)

I'll put him on. It's Brian.

Paul quickly takes the phone.

PAUL

Hi Brian ... sure ... About two then? ... Ok ... See you then!

SHARYN

I didn't know what to say to him. What did he want?

PAUL

Wants me to drop by at two for a check-up and chat. Want to come?

SHARYN

Actually, yes I do! Thanks!

40.   INT. DOCTOR'S OFFICE

Brian, Sharyn & Paul are chatting together.
Brian is a small man, balding and with a very kind face. An
ex school mate of Paul's.

DR BRIAN WILLIAMS

It's been three months since I saw you last.

PAUL

Really?

DR BRIAN WILLIAMS

According to my records. Let's take a look at you.

Brian puts a bright light against Paul and looks into his eyes

DR BRIAN WILLIAMS (cont'd)

I thought you'd be looking a little worse for wear by this time.

He catches Sharyn's concerned look.

SHARYN

What do you mean Brian?

DR BRIAN WILLIAMS

If I was looking at him for the first time today without my previous
knowledge ... I'd say he looks fine.

SHARYN

(teary)

Is he getting better?

DR BRIAN WILLIAMS

I'll take some blood and get pathology to let me know what's really happening.

PAUL

Wow!

DR BRIAN WILLIAMS

Have you been doing anything different or eating anything unusual?

PAUL

Well I quit my job and took up fishing.

DR BRIAN WILLIAMS

Fishing?

PAUL

I guess I'm eating a lot more fresh fish is all.

DR BRIAN WILLIAMS

Well whatever it is you're doing keep doing it! There's a lot we don't know about cancer in general, and if something is working. And not going against medical principals. Who am I to say anything?

Sharyn looks over at Paul and squeezes his hand.

A telephone on Brian's desk rings.

DR BRIAN WILLIAMS (cont'd)

No calls at the moment ... What! ... I see ... Thanks for letting me know ... 'bye.

Brian looks up at Paul.

DR BRIAN WILLIAMS (cont'd)

You remember an old school mate of ours, Raymond Willis? Dropped dead at his office an hour ago.

PAUL

The lawyer?

DR BRIAN WILLIAMS

Yep. Had a stroke.

PAUL

He wasn't a friend of mine.

SHARYN

Wasn't he the one who did the dirty on you about ten years back?

PAUL

(smiling)

At least I outlived that bastard!

DR BRIAN WILLIAMS
The funeral is on Wednesday if you're interested.

PAUL
I think I'll pass!

41.   **EXT. A CITY STREET**

Paul and Sharyn walk arm in arm towards their car.

SHARYN
Oh babe, how good is this?

PAUL
You bet ya!

42.   **INT. PAUL'S BED**

Paul is tossing wildly in the middle of a nightmare.

Cross cut dissolve to a dream sequence.

Paul has a gun to Raymond's head and is threatening to pull the trigger.

PAUL
You never said sorry ....

RAYMOND
(pleading)
Don't kill me, please!

Paul releases the safety switch and takes aim.

RAYMOND (cont'd)
What about my kids! Who's going to look after them!

The gun goes off.

PAUL
(coldly)
Should have thought of that before!

Paul fires the gun again.

The scene dissolves from the dream back to reality.

Sharyn has woken up and nudged Paul in the ribs to stop shaking the bed.

Sharyn notices he is drenched in sweat.

Paul wakes up.

SHARYN
(softly)
What were you dreaming of?

PAUL
(drowsily)
Sorry babe, did I disturb you?

Sharyn gets up and brings a towel back to the bed.

SHARYN
Here, dry yourself off.

Paul takes the towel and wipes himself.

PAUL
Thanks, I can't remember anything.

Paul goes straight back to sleep as Sharyn watches him with a concerned look on her face.

43.   **EXT. THE FISHING PIER**

Paul sees Chris and quietly goes next to him.

PAUL
Kalimera!

Chris looks up quite startled.

CHRIS
You nearly scared the life out of me!

PAUL
Sorry.

CHRIS
It's OK! Late today huh?

PAUL
Big night!

Paul gets his fishing gear out and starts baiting up.

PAUL (cont'd)
Celebration!

CHRIS
Don't bother with the fish this morning ... All on holiday.

PAUL
Oh!

CHRIS
What's your good news?

PAUL
The doctor thinks I'm no worse off than three months back.

CHRIS
(laughing)
No worse off!

PAUL
Well yeh. He thinks I'm doing something right.

They both laugh out loud and the other fishermen look over at them suspiciously.

44.   INT. PAUL'S KITCHEN AREA

Paul and Sharyn are eating dinner at the kitchen table. Paul opens a bottle of red wine.

PAUL
Remember this bottle?

SHARYN
Not really. Where did we get it from?

PAUL
That vineyard in the Yarra Valley last year.

SHARYN
Now I do.

Paul pours two glasses and they are seen enjoying each other's company in joyful conversation throughout the meal.

45.   EXT. THE FISHING PIER

Paul wanders down and notices that Chris isn't there.
Paul waits about an hour and then leaves.

46.   EXT. THE FISHING PIER THE NEXT MORNING

Paul wanders down again and still Chris is not there. He sees a new man fishing where Chris used to be. They exchange a glance.

47.   INT. CHRIS'S HOUSE

Paul is seen parking his car outside of Chris's house and knocking on the door.

PAUL
(calling out)
Chris! Come on. Chris!

As there is no reply Paul writes a note and sticks it in the door. Paul walks back to his car.

48.   INT. PAUL'S KITCHEN AREA

Paul and Sharyn are chatting over a coffee.

SHARYN
So, where do you think he's gone?

PAUL
I don't really know him that well.

SHARYN

I suppose so.

49.   **INT. RESTAURANT**

Paul, Sharyn, Andy and Rita and enjoying a night out.

RiTA

We were thinking of going to Bali in a month's time for some R&R.

SHARYN

Sounds great! How long for?

RITA

About ten days.

SHARYN

Want some company?

RITA

Sure!

PAUL

If we're not intruding …

ANDY

Don't be silly. It will be like the old days!

PAUL

Too easy then!

Paul's mobile goes off and he takes the call.

PAUL (cont'd)

Yellow!

Split screen we can see Chris in a hospital ward.
CHRIS
(out of shot)
It's me … Chris!

PAUL

Hi Chris. Where've you been?

CHRIS

(out of shot)

My sister had a car accident about a week ago … We are now going to take
her off life support.

PAUL

I'm so sorry!

CHRIS

(out of shot)

Yes. Maybe I have to go back to Greece to settle affairs there too.

PAUL

Sure. Is there anything I can do?

CHRIS

(out of shot)

Maybe. The house needs a look in from time to time.

PAUL

Of course.

CHRIS

(out of shot)

I'll let you know when I go. OK?

PAUL

Sure. Speak soon!

CHRIS

(out of shot)

Bye!

SHARYN

(sarcastically)

So that was Chris?

PAUL

His sister was in an accident...

SHARYN

That's not good.

ANDY

Who's Chris?

PAUL

A fishing buddy.

ANDY

Oh you've never mentioned him before.

PAUL

I met him three months ago when I took up fishing.

Paul quickly saves Chris's number on his mobile phone.

50.   INT. PAUL'S KITCHEN AREA

Paul and Sharyn chatting.

SHARYN

He sounds like your new best friend.

PAUL

Who?

SHARYN

Chris!

PAUL

I'm not sure what he is to me. I like him and we seem to get on pretty well.

SHARYN

There's something about him. I can't put my finger on it.

PAUL

Come on!

SHARYN

You know I'm a good judge of people.

PAUL

He's OK!

51.	**EXT. THE FISHING PIER**

Paul wanders down to his regular spot, acknowledges the other Greek fishermen and even smiles at the new-comer.

Casts a line in and stares out to the sea.

52.	**INT. PAUL'S KITCHEN AREA**

Paul is alone reading a newspaper when his mobile phone rings.

PAUL

Yellow!

CHRIS

(split screen .. Chris is at the airport)
It's me ... Chris!

PAUL

How are you?

CHRIS

(split screen .. Chris is at the airport)
I'm on my way to Athens. Be back in two weeks.

PAUL

I'm sorry about your sister.

CHRIS

(split screen .. Chris is at the airport)
Me too. I left a key under the mat if you wouldn't mind feeding my cat every couple of days. I hope it's not too much trouble for you?

PAUL

I'd be glad to do it. After what we've been through.

CHRIS

(split screen .. Chris is at the airport)
Good! See you in two weeks or something like that.
PAUL
OK. Have a safe trip.

Paul goes back to his paper and starts to do a puzzle with his pen. He suddenly gets his mobile phone and puts in a reminder for every second day to go to Chris's house.

53.	INT. PAUL'S HOUSE	LATER THAT NIGHT AT DINNER

SHARYN

I spoke to Rita today about Bali.

PAUL

When is that supposed to happen?

SHARYN

Pretty soon.

PAUL

What, two or three weeks' time?

SHARYN

I'd say three weeks. Is that OK?

PAUL

(relieved)

Should be fine. I promised Chris to feed his cat.

SHARYN

Chris again!

Paul glares at Sharyn and she turns away from him.

SHARYN (cont'd)

He better not interfere with our plans.

PAUL

(somewhat annoyed)

It will be Ok

SHARYN

We'll see. Anyway I'm booking the tickets tomorrow!

54.	EXT. THE FISHING PIER

Paul catches a fish.

55.	INT/EXT. CHRIS'S HOUSE

Paul finds the key and goes inside to see plenty of cat food on the kitchen table. He finds the cat bowl outside the back door and puts the food into it, pours some water into another bowl and calls out to the cat.

PAUL

Puss! Here puss!

Nothing happens so after a while Paul leaves.

A black cat sidles up to Paul as he delivers the food.

PAUL
You're a beautiful cat.

Paul watches the cat eating for about five minutes and then leaves.

57.   **INT. PAUL'S KITCHEN AREA**

Paul and Sharyn have a coffee together.

SHARYN
I'm sorry if I haven't asked how you were feeling.

PAUL
Not too bad.

SHARYN
What does that mean?

PAUL
Well, I was going to tell you that when I woke up this morning I was a bit dizzy is all.

SHARYN
(concerned)
Oh babe! How are you feeling now?

PAUL
Strangely better. It did give me a scare alright!

SHARYN
I'll bet it did!

Sharyn goes and gives Paul a decent hug and kisses him.

PAUL
I actually was starting to believe I'd beaten this thing.

SHARYN
Poor baby.

PAUL
Gave me a lesson in grounding.

SHARYN
You're doing unbelievably well if you ask me.

PAUL
Thanks babe. You've been ... I mean are, great.

They go back to their drinks in silence.

PAUL (cont'd)
When are we booked for Bali?

SHARYN

In a fortnight. The twenty fifth. You'll be OK won't you?

PAUL

I'm sure I will. I better text Chris that we'll be away.

SHARYN

Mmm!

Paul gets out his phone and texts madly.

Paul and Sharyn are seen watching the news on TV as Paul's mobile tweaks. Paul looks at the text and texts back a reply.

PAUL

It's Chris. He will be home next Wednesday. I guess I can stop worrying.

SHARYN

That's good dear. You might even get a fish or two with him before we fly out.

PAUL

Yeah! That'd be good.

---

58.   EXT. THE FISHING PIER

Paul wanders down and sees Chris. They exchange a smile as Paul sets up his gear.

PAUL

How did it all go?

CHRIS

It's sort of done. Thanks for the house stuff.

PAUL

Pleasure. Glad I was on the spot.

CHRIS

So you're going away next week?

PAUL

Yeah! To Bali.

CHRIS

Nice!

PAUL

Can we talk about one more before I go?

CHRIS

What!

Some of the other fishermen look up as Chris raised his voice. They soon go back to their own business.

CHRIS (cont'd)
Who's this one then?

PAUL
Barry Connors.

CHRIS
What did he do to you?

PAUL
He was my best friend going through school and when I got married to my
first wife, he cheated on me with her.

CHRIS
That's not enough to kill him!

PAUL
Well, he cheated on her too!

CHRIS
How?

PAUL
She left me to be with him in Sydney, but he was already engaged!

CHRIS
These things happen …

PAUL
The relationship I had had with both of them was over. She took up the
drink and committed suicide a few years later...

CHRIS
Another crime of passion.

PAUL
He's a policeman!

CHRIS
I have never liked them either.

PAUL
So you'll help?

CHRIS
Why not. Same as before, poison?

PAUL
I guess.

CHRIS
I still have enough Miraios funnily enough.

PAUL
Great!

CHRIS
I suggest we drive to Sydney, you have his address?

PAUL

Oh yes. I'm prepared.

CHRIS

(laughing)

You're getting good at this!

PAUL

When do you think?

CHRIS

Look I actually need your help again this afternoon for about two hours.

PAUL

Ok, what time?

CHRIS

Three O'clock would be perfect.

PAUL

Can we talk about Sydney then too?

CHRIS

Sure.

They quietly go back to their fishing and pretty soon everyone on the pier is having some success.

---

59.   **INT. PAUL'S KITCHEN AREA**

Paul is cooking fish for lunch with Sharyn.

PAUL

Chris needs a hand this afternoon so I'll go round there about three if that's Ok?

SHARYN

What does he need you for?

PAUL

He didn't say but it's probably to hold a ladder or something like that.

SHARYN

Don't forget the dinner party tonight at seven.

PAUL

Thanks. I'll keep an eye on the time.

SHARYN

If we leave here by six thirty I'll be happy.

PAUL

Too easy.

Paul drives up to Chris's place and checks his watch, five to three, knocks on the door.

Chris greets him with a big smile.

CHRIS

I like a man who knows that time is important.

PAUL

You said three. I actually need to be home by about five thirty if that's Ok?

CHRIS

We better not waste any time then.

Chris ushers Paul into a large garage area where two cars are parked.

Chris points to the other car.

CHRIS (cont'd)

My sister's car.

PAUL

Oh.

Chris points to some heavily tinted windows that each have a round hole in the middle of them.

PAUL (cont'd)

What do you want them for?

CHRIS

My uncle in Athens is having some trouble with a bad man from here.

PAUL

(somewhat shocked)

And...

CHRIS

(handing Paul a screwdriver)

Please hold this.

Chris and Paul manage to take the window out and replace it with the tinted one.

PAUL

You were saying.

CHRIS

Well, he paid me fifteen thousand dollars to get rid of him.

PAUL

Wow!

CHRIS

Let's get the other window done.

PAUL

Ok.

Chris and Paul complete the job and Paul looks at his watch.

PAUL (cont'd)

That was easy it's only twenty to four.

CHRIS

Good! Get in! You drive, I'll tell you where to go.

PAUL

Wait a minute.

CHRIS

(laughing)

A tough killer you are!

Paul is quite silent as Chris gets a rifle with a silencer and telescopic sights attached.

CHRIS (cont'd)

(proudly)

Brand new. It will be fun.

PAUL

(nervously)

I don't want to stuff it up.

CHRIS

Of course you won't. What do you have to lose?

PAUL

What do I have to do?

CHRIS

Drive where I say so and park. I pull the trigger and then I tell you to drive slowly away. Easy!

Paul is a little shaken, but also excited.

PAUL

When do we go?

CHRIS

In five minutes!

Chris laughs as Paul gets into the driver's seat while Chris opens the garage door.

Paul backs the car out very nervously.

Chris closes the garage door and hops into the back seat with the gun and a box of shells.

PAUL

(a little shocked)

Oh my God!

CHRIS

Alexis always goes to his club in Richmond around four thirty. Swan Street.

PAUL

(nervously)

Shit!

CHRIS

By the way he has two bodyguards as well.

PAUL

I'm going to throw up!

Chris laughs loudly and directs Paul down the street.

61.   INT/EXT. SWAN STREET

The Ford with Paul at the wheel glides into Swan Street. Chris points out the club.

CHRIS

That's the place over there. Just park out front and we wait.

Paul does as he is told and the two men wait in silence for about fifteen minutes. Suddenly Chris see Alexis and two of his body guards wander up to the front door of the club.

Chris takes aim and puts two bullets into the head of Alexis and he drops down dead.

The two guards pull out their guns as Chris hits them both as well. Quietly Chris taps a shaking Paul on the shoulder.

CHRIS (cont'd)

That was a bonus. Drive slowly away and keep driving the same way we came. Ok?

PAUL

Jesus Christ!

Paul takes a deep breath and does as he is told and the car goes out of sight.

62.   INT. CHRIS'S KITCHEN

Chris gets Paul a drink and has one himself.

CHRIS

Ouzo! Always after a job!

Paul gulps the drink down and coughs wildly.

CHRIS (cont'd)

Easy does it.

PAUL

We just killed three men!

CHRIS
Yes! You did very well if I may say that.

PAUL
Really?

CHRIS
I knew you would be alright.

PAUL
Then you knew more than me!

Chris pulls out a wad of notes and hands it to Paul.

PAUL (cont'd)
What's this then?

CHRIS
Five thousand dollars. Your share from my uncle.

The two men look at each other.

PAUL
(face lighting up)
Too easy.

CHRIS
(smiling)
You earned it! Tell Sharyn you won it playing the machines.

Paul looks at his watch and stuffs the money into his jacket.

PAUL
Jesus! I really have to go!

Paul bolts for the door and drives nervously home.

63. **INT. PAUL'S HOUSE**

Paul scrambles up the stairs and heads for the shower.

SHARYN
(out of shot)
That you babe?

PAUL
Sorry, I know I'm a bit late.

SHARYN
(out of shot)
That's Ok. Have a good time?

PAUL
I'll tell you all about it after I shower.

SHARYN
Ok.

*Paul dumps the money on his dresser, strips and goes into
a hot shower. We see him totally enjoying it.*

*Sharyn sees the money on the dresser and comes in to the
shower room.*

SHARYN (cont'd)
What's with all the money?

PAUL
After working on his car he took me to his club for a drink and we won it
on the pokies.

SHARYN
Good for you!

PAUL
Yeh a bit lucky.

SHARYN
I'd say.

64.   INT. PAUL'S CAR

Paul and Sharyn are driving to their dinner party.

PAUL
I was thinking we might use that money to upgrade our tickets to business
class. What do you think?

SHARYN
Could be fun.

65.   INT. ESTELLE'S HOME   EVENING

*Estelle is hosting a dinner party. Paul and Sharyn are seen
mingling with people as Estelle, comes over for a chat.*

*Estelle is a trim, good looking fifty year old, blond and
dressed to impress. She is wearing jewellery that indicates
her to be wealthy.*

SHARYN
Hi Estelle!

ESTELLE
Hi Sharyn, Paul. It's been a while.

PAUL
You've got a beautiful home.

ESTELLE
Thanks! I heard you'd retired.

PAUL
About six months back.

ESTELLE
So what are you doing with yourself?

PAUL
I kill people!

Sharyn gets very flustered and embarrassed.

SHARYN
Of course he doesn't! He spends his time fishing!

They all laugh.

ESTELLE
Catch anything?

PAUL
Sometimes.

ESTELLE
Oh well enjoy yourselves I must circulate.

Estelle goes off and Sharyn glares at Paul.

SHARYN
What a thing to say!

PAUL
I thought it was funny.

SHARYN
Well it wasn't!

PAUL
Sorry babe.

The night goes on with small talk and cocktail drinking.

PAUL (cont'd)
I need a bit of air. You don't mind if I take my drink outside for a bit?

SHARYN
No. You go and I'll chat on.

PAUL
Thanks.

*Paul wanders out onto the patio and leans over the railing
in deep thought.*
Estelle sees him go and soon follows him.

ESTELLE
Had enough eh?

PAUL
Oh hi Estelle. I needed a bit of air.

ESTELLE
It can be like that.

Estelle looks at him intently.

ESTELLE (cont'd)
I may not know much in this world, but when I hear the truth I do recognise it.

PAUL
What do you mean?

ESTELLE
Your other life!

PAUL
I was just joking.

ESTELLE
I don't think so. What do you charge?

Estelle and Paul glare at each other in a nervous silence.

ESTELLE (cont'd)
I can be trusted.

Paul pretends to be suave "jokes" to Estelle.

PAUL
Twenty five thousand dollars! Half up front the rest after the job completes!

Estelle looks shocked.

ESTELLE
Wow! I was right wasn't I?

Paul smiles, trying to put on a James Bond appearance of some indifference.

ESTELLE (cont'd)
My life is veneer.

PAUL
Ben? I thought you were happy?

ESTELLE
Think again!

Paul, with a somewhat worried look on his face, as if the joke has gone too far, turns away from Estelle and faces the garden.

PAUL
We fly to Bali on Tuesday for ten days.

ESTELLE
What about now?

PAUL
Ring me on the pretence you found my pen and I'll know you have the money and I'll arrange to come over when Ben's home.

                    ESTELLE
                    That simple?

                     PAUL
              (trying to shock and impress)
      What would you like? Guns, knives, heart attack?

                    ESTELLE
        Heart attack would be great for the insurance.

                     PAUL
                Too easy! Call me!

Paul wanders back to the party with Estelle alone in the night air pondering what just happened.

66.   RICHMOND POLICE STATION

Two detectives are going over the shooting incident.

                  DETECTIVE 1
            Nobody seems to know anything.

                  DETECTIVE 2
        The Greeks know better than to talk to us.

                  DETECTIVE 1
              What do you reckon?

                  DETECTIVE 2
We could put a tab on some people he knew and had dealings with. I have a few contacts. He must have pissed a few people off in his line of business.

                  DETECTIVE 1
         Let me know if you get anything.

                  DETECTIVE 2
                Of course.

67.   INT. PAUL'S BED

Paul is having another nightmare, tossing and turning quite violently

Shot dissolves into a dream sequence.

Paul is in a James Bond dinner suit, holding a knife to Raymond's throat.

                   RAYMOND
                  (pleading)
             I can get a lot of money.

                     PAUL
                   (suave)
             I don't want your money.

RAYMOND

What do you want?

Paul sinks the knife deep into Raymond's throat with blood gushing everywhere.

PAUL

Revenge!

Shot dissolves back to reality.

Sharyn nudges Paul, turns the light on and gets up to get a towel from the bathroom.

SHARYN

(calling out)

Are you awake?

Paul opens his eyes and looks at the clock which says two thirty.

PAUL

(gruffly)

I am now!

Sharyn comes back and hands him a towel.

Paul takes the towel and wipes himself down. He seems quite embarrassed.

SHARYN

Too much late night eating and drinking.

PAUL

(relieved)

Must be.

Sharyn turns off the light and they both go back to sleep.

---

68.   INT. PAUL'S KITCHEN AREA

It's Sunday night and the phone rings. Sharyn picks it up.

SHARYN

Sharyn here … Oh hi Estelle … yes a lovely party wasn't it … you found Paul's pen … I'll tell him to drop round to pick it up … When we get back from Bali … Ok will do, love to Ben … Bye!

PAUL

Who was that?

SHARYN

Estelle, she found your pen. I didn't know you lost one.

PAUL

No need to worry you about little things eh?

SHARYN

I guess not.

PAUL

I'll drop by after fishing and get it.

69.	INT. PAUL'S HOUSE	LATER THAT NIGHT

Paul rings Chris.

PAUL

Hi Chris, you OK?

CHRIS

(out of shot)

Another job?

PAUL

Paying one too! Could you bring that bottle tomorrow morning?

CHRIS

(out of shot)

Good for you. Need help?

PAUL

No, it's best I do this one on my own. We'll still share the profits.

70.	EXT. ESTELLE'S PLACE	MORNING

Paul, still in his tracksuit, drives up to Estelle's place. It is around eight thirty in the morning.

Paul puts his gloves on and smears the poison.

Paul knocks on the door.

Ben, Mid-sixties, grey hair, medium height and build, dressed in a business suit, answers the door.

BEN

Hi Paul, Estelle said you might drop by. I'll get her. Estelle!

PAUL

(shaking Ben's hand firmly)

Thanks Ben, nice party!

BEN

What's with the gloves?

PAUL

Dermatitis! I've just been fishing as well.

BEN

Catch any?

PAUL

Not this morning. Off to Bali tomorrow.

Estelle comes to the door in a dressing gown with a package and a pen.

ESTELLE
Here's your pen and some articles for Sharyn.

PAUL
Thanks Estelle. We'll catch up in a couple of weeks when we get back.

Ben wanders back inside.

ESTELLE
(whispering)
What about our arrangement?

PAUL
Already done.

ESTELLE
What!?

PAUL
You'll see, in about four hours' time. Make sure you are with a friend. Ok?

ESTELLE
(still in shock)
Ok.

PAUL
See you later.

ESTELLE
Bye.

---

71.   INT. CHRIS'S KITCHEN   LATER THAT MORNING

Paul unwraps the package on Chris's kitchen table and a stack of hundred dollar bills is seen.

CHRIS
(smiling)
Just like old times.

PAUL
Not for me!

They count out the money into two piles.

PAUL (cont'd)
Could you hold onto mine till I get back?

CHRIS
Of course. Partner.

They both smile at each other.

---

72.   INT. PAUL'S HOUSE   LATER THAT NIGHT

Paul and Sharyn are enjoying a steak dinner alone with a bottle of wine.

PAUL

Our last meal.

SHARYN

Don't say that! You'll put the mozz on us!

The phone rings and Paul answers it.

PAUL

Yellow! You don't say … I just saw him this morning, he did look a little pale
… Thanks for letting me know … Bye!

SHARYN

What was all that?

PAUL

Ben has had a stroke at work and was dead before the ambulance came!

SHARYN

Oh poor Estelle!

PAUL

Yeh.

SHARYN

I'll send her an SMS. She'll understand we are travelling.

PAUL

Good idea! We are all pretty fragile.

SHARYN

I know! By the way I managed to upgrade our tickets to First Class.

PAUL

First Class! I said Business! How much did that set us back?

SHARYN

All of that five thousand.

PAUL

It's done now. I'll bet Andy and Rita will be a bit surprised?

SHARYN

Let them! They are always bragging about one thing and another.

PAUL

I see.

*Sharyn gets out her mobile phone and starts to SMS. Paul
goes back to his steak.*

73.   INT. AIRPORT TERMINAL

*Paul, Sharyn, Andy and Rita arrive at the airport booking
office. There are plenty of people and the queues are long.
Paul and Sharyn head off to the empty queue of First Class.
Rita calls to them.*

RITA

Not that queue unless you're travelling in style.

SHARYN

(smiling)
That's what we're doing.

RITA

What Business Class?

SHARYN

No! First Class! Never done it before and I guess it's now or never.

RITA

We'll come and visit, if they let us.

SHARYN

Of course. French Champagne and lobster is on the menu too I believe.

RITA

(friendly)
Bitch!

They all share a laugh as Paul and Sharyn go straight to the front and watch as Andy and Rita are moving slowly in three rows of humans.

74.   **INT. AEROPLANE FIRST CLASS AREA**

Paul and Sharyn are settling into the big comfortable chairs as the flight attendant arrives with a bottle of French champagne and some nibbles.

FLIGHT ATTENDANT

The special for dinner is a Canadian bisque, followed by a lobster Californe, salads and herb breads.

SHARYN

That sounds wonderful!

PAUL

Yeh! I'll have that as well, thanks.

FLIGHT ATTENDANT

It should be ready in about forty minutes. If there's anything else please let me know.

PAUL

(smiling)
Will do!

The flight attendant leaves them as Andy and Rita poke their heads around the corner.

ANDY

Just wanted to see how the other half were living.

PAUL
Too easy! Here try some of this bubbly.

Paul hands over his champagne glass and watches as Andy and Rita take a sip.

RITA
Not bad at all! We should travel like this too!

ANDY
Sure!

SHARYN
(laughing)
It is pretty good!

Paul fills up their glass and they all have a bit of a chat as well as testing out the seats.
The flight attendant comes back.

FLIGHT ATTENDANT
I'm afraid you will all have to return to your seats now. You're not allowed up here you know.

Andy and Rita smile at Paul and Sharyn as they head back to the Economy section.

RITA
Enjoy it guys! See you in Bali!

SHARYN
That's the plan!

After a short while the dinner is served and it looks stunning.

SHARYN (cont'd)
Real cutlery.

PAUL
At these prices what did you expect?

SHARYN
I thought with security such a big deal these days, it might have been plastic.

PAUL
Good point! Obviously we are a low threat!

They both chuckle and look very satisfied with themselves.

SHARYN
The look in Rita's eyes was worth every penny!

PAUL
You bet ya!

Paul and Sharyn are seen sleeping in their comfortable first class chairs.

Camera dissolves into a dream sequence.

Paul is again in a dinner suit. A smoking gun in his hand.

Ben is slumped in a corner.

BEN
(croaking)
What did I ever do to you?

PAUL
(casually)
Nothing Ben, it's only business.

BEN
You bastard! I'll be waiting for you on the other side!

PAUL
Whatever you say, Ben.

Camera dissolves back to reality.

Paul wakes up in a fright, realizes he is soaked through again and gets up and goes to the toilets.

Paul comes back to his eat. Sharyn is still asleep.

Paul rings for the flight attendant, who comes by.

PAUL
Could I get a whisky please?

FLIGHT ATTENDANT
(whispering)
Sure! Can't sleep?

Paul nods and the flight attendant goes away. The air hostess soon comes back with the drink and a small packet of nuts.

FLIGHT ATTENDANT
If you need another, give me a call ...

PAUL
Thanks! Will do.

Paul quietly sculls the drink as a worried look of deep concern comes over him.

---

75.   **INT. PAUL'S KITCHEN AREA**

Paul and Sharyn are having a coffee with their suitcases dumped on the floor of the kitchen.

PAUL
First decent coffee for ten days.

SHARYN
You know you're addicted to the stuff.

PAUL

Probably kill me!

They smile tenderly and knowingly at each other.

SHARYN

Oh babe, it was a wonderful holiday.

PAUL

Absolutely!

The phone answering machine is flashing and Sharyn goes over to it.

SHARYN

Here goes!

Sharyn pushes the button and ten messages spew out. Most notable was Estelle.

ESTELLE

(out of shot, voice on answering machine)
Hi guys I'm wondering when you're back if Paul could drop by to help me with some of Ben's papers. Call me!

SHARYN

That's a bit strange for her to ask you don't you think?

PAUL

(casually)
Why don't you call her tomorrow and I'll drop over in a few days' time.

SHARYN

Ok, good idea. I don't think I could face anything but my own bed right now.

PAUL

Sounds good.

76.   INT. PAUL'S KITCHEN AREA

Sharyn is making some lunch and Paul is reading the paper. The phone rings. Sharyn answers it.

SHARYN

Hello.

ESTELLE

(split screen)
Hi Sharyn, when did you get back?

SHARYN

(split screen)
Oh Estelle, I'm so sorry about Ben you poor dear.

ESTELLE

(split screen)

Thanks it has been a rough time. I was hoping Paul could drop by and go through some of Ben's papers relating to his marketing, as I don't understand all the jargon.

SHARYN

(split screen)

Of course he will! When will be a good time?

ESTELLE

(split screen)

Is two today convenient?

SHARYN

(split screen)

I'll make sure he gets there.

ESTELLE

(split screen)

Thanks Sharyn.

SHARYN

(split screen)

Is there anything I can do?

ESTELLE

(split screen)

I'll give you a call in a couple of weeks when some of the dust has settled and we'll have coffee. Ok?

SHARYN

Sounds good. You stay well dear.

ESTELLE

(out of shot)

Bye.

Paul looks up from his paper and smiles at Sharyn.

PAUL

She's not my type you know.

SHARYN

What a difficult time for her.

PAUL

I'll get dressed and be there by two. Not sure what I can do exactly, but whatever.

SHARYN

You're a good man.

Paul wanders upstairs as Sharyn thoughtfully goes back to her lunch preparations.

Paul knocks on the door and Estelle smiles at him and ushers him inside where a tall man is sitting at a dining room table.

ESTELLE

Hi Paul, this is David.

DAVID

(getting up and extending a hand)
Estelle has told me a lot about you, nice to meet.

PAUL

Hi!

Looking a bit confused, Paul gets Estelle's eye.

PAUL (cont'd)

What's going on Estelle?

ESTELLE

David is my lover. Has been for the past five years.

PAUL

I see.

ESTELLE

Ben and I were only show ponies there was little love there, I can assure you.

PAUL

You don't have to explain.

ESTELLE

(putting a package in front of Paul)
There's twenty five thousand dollars.

PAUL

Ok.

ESTELLE

We would like to be together and he has a wife.

PAUL

I see.

ESTELLE

(a bit concerned)
It's ok isn't it?

Paul is a bit flushed in the face.

PAUL

I guess so.

ESTELLE
(relieved)
Paul you're a gem!

PAUL
(to David)
When and where? Do you have a photograph?

DAVID
I'm going to Sydney next Wednesday for two days at a business
conference. If the Thursday could be alright it will be perfect.

*David hands an envelope to Paul. Paul opens it and a photo
of an attractive middle aged woman, with an address on
the back, falls out onto the table.*

DAVID (cont'd)
Is that what you need?

PAUL
On Thursday I'll pay her a visit then.

*The three of them go very silent. Paul picks up the envelope
and the package and heads for the door.*

PAUL (cont'd)
See you Estelle, David.

ESTELLE
Thanks Paul, and mum's the word from here on.

PAUL
(smiling)
You take care.

*Paul is seen with a wry smile on his face as he drives over
to Chris's house.*

---

78.   INT/EXT CHRIS'S HOUSE   MINUTES LATER

*Paul knocks on the door. The cat comes in from the garden
and rubs against him.*

PAUL
(stroking the cat)
How you doing?

Chis opens the door and smiles as the cat races inside.

CHRIS
You didn't say you were coming over?

PAUL
Is it Ok?

CHRIS
Sure! Come on in! The police just paid me a visit too.

PAUL

Shit! How did it go?

CHRIS

(laughing)

I have a record and they know nothing that's for sure.

79.   **INT. CHRIS'S KITCHEN**

Paul goes straight to the kitchen table and lays the money on it.

CHRIS

You have been busy.

PAUL

Money from the last job and half of a new one.

CHRIS

This is a good business. Money and no tax! I like it!

PAUL

It's complicated, but I could use your help on the next one.

CHRIS

Of course! When is it to be?

PAUL

Next Thursday, and it's a woman!

CHRIS

Business is business, as they say.

PAUL

I have a photograph and an address.

CHRIS

Let me see.

Chris examines the photo and looks at the address carefully.

CHRIS (cont'd)

She's not bad looking!

PAUL

I know! What do you think?

CHRIS

It has to be Thursday for a reason?

PAUL

Yeh! Husband interstate.

Chris thinks it over for a bit.

CHRIS

After fishing we go over there early in the morning and wait till she gets her morning paper.

PAUL

Put the poison over the wrapper?

CHRIS

We have to make sure no one else picks it up!

PAUL

Oh yeah! That would be terrible!

The two men look at each other and then burst out laughing.

CHRIS

I have an idea about all this money too.

PAUL

Yeh?

CHRIS

A friend of mine has a boat for sale. I could buy it and we could fish a lot better.

PAUL

Sounds like a plan! Just do it!

CHRIS

Ok!

80.   EXT. DAVID'S HOUSE

Paul and Chris are sitting in Paul's car outside David's house. It is early morning.

A small van goes past and we see a paper being flung onto the lawn.

Chris gets out of the car and we see him pick up the paper and smear the poison over the wrapper. He then places the paper neatly next to the front door of the house.

Chris goes back to Paul's car and they wait and watch.

CHRIS

Are you sure she's home?

PAUL

No idea! I've never met her before.

CHRIS

Let's see what happens

After an hour the front door opens and a man in a dressing gown steps out and picks up the paper and goes inside again.

CHRIS (cont'd)

Who was that? I thought you said...

PAUL

That's not her husband either! I have no idea who that is!

CHRIS

I think we better get out of here.

PAUL

Good idea!

Paul revs the engine and the car goes out of sight.

81.   INT. PAUL'S KITCHEN AREA

Paul comes into the kitchen area as Sharyn is preparing a coffee.

SHARYN

Hi babe! Have some fun?

PAUL

Yeh it was ok.

SHARYN

You don't sound convincing! Coffee?

PAUL

Thanks! It was bloody cold out there is all and the fish weren't biting.

SHARYN

You poor dear.

Sharyn starts to make some breakfast for them both and gets some plates out on the table.

PAUL

Chris is getting a boat soon, so it will be a lot better.

SHARYN

How much will it cost you?

PAUL

I bet he won't charge me.

SHARYN

Better not! Too many expenses at the moment.

PAUL

It will be ok, babe.

82.   INT. PAUL'S HOUSE   LATER IN THE DAY

The phone rings and Paul picks it up.

PAUL

Yellow!

DR BRIAN WILLIAMS

(out of shot)

Hi Paul, it's Brian!

PAUL

Hi mate!

DR BRIAN WILLIAMS

(out of shot)

How you feeling?

PAUL

A bit tired but I have been fishing this morning.

DR BRIAN WILLIAMS

(out of shot)

No other aches and pains?

PAUL

Surprisingly not! That's good isn't it?

DR BRIAN WILLIAMS

(out of shot)

Well yes it is. How about you drop by towards five thirty, if that's OK, and
I'll take some more blood. See what's happening.

PAUL

Sounds good to me. Catch you then!

DR BRIAN WILLIAMS

(out of shot)

See you then!

Paul hangs up the phone as Sharyn comes into the room.

SHARYN

Who was that?

PAUL

Brian! Wants me to drop by this arvo.

SHARYN

What time?

PAUL

Five thirty! Want to come?

SHARYN

Ok!

83. **INT. DOCTOR'S OFFICE**

Brian is rolling up Paul's arm, ready to take some blood.

DR BRIAN WILLIAMS

I've got Max Williams waiting to rush this through at pathology down the
corridor.

SHARYN
I thought it took a few days?

DR BRIAN WILLIAMS
Usually, but I've pulled a favour.

PAUL
Let's do it then.

Brian gets a sample and labels it. He calls out to his receptionist.

DR BRIAN WILLIAMS
Betty could you please run it down to Max he's waiting for it.

RECEPTIONIST
Sure doctor!

The receptionist leaves and there are other people waiting to go in to see the doctor.

DR BRIAN WILLIAMS
(to Paul and Sharyn)
If you wouldn't mind waiting it will be about an hour.

PAUL
No problem.

Paul and Sharyn sit in the waiting room. Paul puts on his mobile phone and sees there are three missed calls from Estelle.
Paul gets up

PAUL (cont'd)
Just going to the loo, babe.

SHARYN
Ok.

Paul walks outside and quickly phones Estelle.

PAUL
It's me.

ESTELLE
(split screen)(pissed off)
What went wrong? I just spoke to David.

PAUL
(split screen)
Calm down!

ESTELLE
(split screen)
Calm down?

PAUL

(split screen)

Some tall guy took the poison.

ESTELLE

(split screen)

Shit! Who is he?

PAUL

(split screen)

No idea! My plan is to go back tonight and finish the job, one way or another!

ESTELLE

(split screen)

Ok! David comes back tomorrow morning.

PAUL

(split screen)

It will be over by then. I got to go!

ESTELLE

(split screen)

Ok!

Paul quickly phones Chris.

Perspiration is seen forming on Paul's forehead, and he wipes it away.

PAUL

(a little stressed)

Hi Chris!

CHRIS

(out of shot)

What's the panic?

PAUL

Sorry, I'm under the pump a bit.

CHRIS

(out of shot)

Take it easy. Let me guess, your friend's wife is still alive and we need to do something about it today before he gets back?

PAUL

(somewhat relieved)

Got it in one! He's not my friend, but I guess that doesn't matter does it?

CHRIS

(out of shot)

I have a plan.

PAUL

Great!

CHRIS
(out of shot)
Everything is fine. Stay calm, our business requires calm, Ok?

PAUL
Thanks, Ok, see you then.

Paul turns off the phone and goes back and sits next to Sharyn in silence. Sharyn is reading a magazine. Paul is just staring into space.

PAUL (cont'd)
(to Sharyn)
It's seven O'clock!

SHARYN
I know!

A scruffy man in a white uniform comes into the room, hands the receptionist a package and then leaves.

The receptionist goes into the doctor's room and both she and a patient come out.

RECEPTIONIST
You can go in now.

Paul and Sharyn quickly go inside the office. Brian is studying the report intently. He looks up after a time.

SHARYN
Good news?

DR BRIAN WILLIAMS
Well it's not bad news!

PAUL
What do you mean?

DR BRIAN WILLIAMS
If I was looking at this report I would say you had six months...

PAUL
That's what you said seven months back! I don't get it!

DR BRIAN WILLIAMS
Neither do I! All I can suggest is what I told you before ... keep doing and eating the same and take each day as a bonus.

They all look at each other in silence.

SHARYN
Wow!

Paul gets up and beckons Sharyn to make a move.

PAUL

Thanks mate it's good to know something's working.

After a pause, Paul leans over and whispers to Sharyn.

PAUL (cont'd)
(quietly)
I promised Chris to give him a hand.

SHARYN

You never mentioned it?

PAUL

Just remembered! Sorry!

DR BRIAN WILLIAMS

Thanks for coming in guys, let's catch each other for a bite sometime.

PAUL

Sure!

Paul and Sharyn leave the office arm in arm.

---

84.   **EXT. DAVID'S HOUSE**   **NEXT MORNING**

Chris and Paul pull up outside David's house. Paul puts on a pair of thin rubber gloves, takes a folder and ink-pad, then walks up to the door and rings the bell.

A woman, David's wife, comes to the door. She has been crying and is a bit upset.

DAVID'S WIFE
(abruptly)
What is it now?

PAUL

Hi I'm sorry to trouble you, but my name is Allan Young from Neighbourhood Watch.

DAVID'S WIFE

So?

PAUL

We are following up a spate of burglaries in this street and would like to eliminate suspects by getting neighbours fingerprints, if you wouldn't mind.

DAVID'S WIFE

And if I say no?

PAUL

Well I guess I'd have to report it and a police officer will come see you tomorrow to find out why.

There is a silence of fifteen seconds.

DAVID'S WIFE

Alright then! What do I have to do?

Paul takes out the ink-pad and opens the lid.

PAUL

Just place one hand on the pad very firmly and then place your hand on the sheet of paper.

She does it quietly.

PAUL (cont'd)

The other hand too.

She does that as well. Paul closes the ink-pad and puts the sheet of paper into a folder.

DAVID'S WIFE

Is that it?

PAUL

That's it! Sorry to trouble you.

She closes the door as Paul walks slowly to the car.
Paul gets in and the car drives off.

85. INT. PAUL'S CAR

CHRIS

It went well, no?

PAUL

(thoughtful)
Very well, I'd say.

Paul gets the car going as smoothly as he can.
Paul drops Chris at his house and the two men exchange meaningful looks

PAUL (cont'd)

Thanks Chris

CHRIS

Good! Have a nice night and don't think about this sort of thing. It's just business.

PAUL

I know.

86. INT. PAUL'S KITCHEN AREA

Paul comes in as Sharyn comes down the stairs.

SHARYN

What did your new best friend want this time?

PAUL

Help with some legal paperwork. His English is not the best.

SHARYN

(sarcastically)

This is not going to be a regular occurrence is it?

PAUL

(firmly)

Hey babe, if I can help I will!

---

87.   EXT. THE FISHING PIER

Paul is sitting next to Chris. They are both fishing.

PAUL

When do you think the new boat will be ready?

CHRIS

He said today, so I'll call him later in the morning.

PAUL

Have you paid him yet?

CHRIS

(laughing)

Not yet! We Greeks don't part with our money that quickly!

PAUL

Too easy!

Paul's mobile rings and he sees it's Estelle.

PAUL (cont'd)

Hi Estelle, you're an early riser?

ESTELLE

(split screen)

Couldn't sleep.

PAUL

(split screen)

Oh!

ESTELLE

(split screen)

(nervous)

David's left me!

PAUL

(split screen)

After all we did?

ESTELLE

(split screen)

The other man you killed was his brother Jake and he blames me.

PAUL

(split screen)

I see.

ESTELLE

(split screen)

It's a mess isn't it?

PAUL

(split screen)

Pretty much! What are you going to do?

ESTELLE

(split screen)

Don't worry, you'll get your money.

PAUL

(split screen)

I mean about now you are alone aren't you?

ESTELLE

(split screen)

My fault! Come by on Friday afternoon and I'll have the rest of your
money.

PAUL

(split screen)

Ok! See you then! Take care!

Chris looks at Paul and smiles, knowingly.

CHRIS

Don't get into anything with her, my friend, nothing good there.

PAUL

(surprised)

Me and Estelle? No way!

CHRIS

Stranger things have happened.

PAUL

Thanks, I'll be on my guard.

Chris smiles and they both go back to their fishing.
Paul is perspiring as drops fall from his forehead.

88.   **EXT/INT. ESTELLE'S PLACE**

Paul comes to the door, knocks and waits.
Estelle comes dressed in a sheer nightie.

ESTELLE

Hi Paul, come in.

Paul looks at Estelle very warily.

ESTELLE (cont'd)
Anything wrong?

PAUL
Look Estelle...

ESTELLE
(Sensing his reluctance)
I'm lonely! It was worth a try.

PAUL
Your own fault you know.

ESTELLE
(pointing to a bag on the kitchen table)
It's all there!

PAUL
Just business Estelle.

ESTELLE
(teary)
What am I going to do now?

PAUL
Plenty of available men around.

ESTELLE
Yeh sure!

Paul quietly takes the bag and leaves without saying anything else.

Paul drives the money over to Chris's house.

89.   EXT. CHRIS'S HOUSE

A boat and a trailer are out the front and Chris is happy to see Paul.

The boat is quite large with two outboard motors at the back. The colour is a striking blue and white with the name "El Greco" printed on one side.

CHRIS
(beaming)
Not bad eh?

Paul hands the money over to Chris and runs his fingers across the woodwork of the boat.

PAUL
(smiling)
Looks OK to me.

       EXT. OUT ON THE NEW BOAT

> *Paul, Sharyn and Chris are enjoying a lunch with a bottle of wine and various Greek foods.*

SHARYN
(to Chris)
So nice of you! Cheaper than going to Greece!

They all laugh.

CHRIS
We'll make a fisherman of you yet.

SHARYN
Don't bet on it!

PAUL
I just love it!

CHRIS
This is the way to live all right.

> *Sharyn looks thoughtfully at Paul, who catches her gaze.*
> *Paul holds her hand, lovingly, under the table.*
> *Chris observes and looks content.*
> *The camera pans out to see other boats on the bay with similar activities.*

91.   **EXT. FINAL SCENE AND CREDITS**

> *Credits start rolling across the screen.*
> *A final scenario takes place where we see Paul on the roof cleaning the leaves.*
> *Sharyn, in a dressing gown, wanders out. She sees the ladder against the roof.*

SHARYN
(to herself)
Did I forget to put it away?

> *Sharyn looks blankly at the ladder and then, struggling, carts it off screen.*
> *Paul crawls over to where the ladder was and gingerly puts one foot over the edge, wriggles it around to find the rung.*
> *Over he goes! Stone dead amongst the blushing red roses.*
> *The neighbour's dog comes over and licks his face.*

THE END

WHERE THERE'S A WILL

<u>**1.   INT. CHICAGO NIGHT CLUB IN 1946**</u>

An all-African American combo are in the middle of a song. A mixed crowd are lapping up the fantastic music.

The keyboard player (Percy Smith) winks at the trumpeter (Lincoln James).

Lincoln is a tall, dark African American, dressed in black pants and a white jacket. He is late twenties and looks very fit, like a boxer. He plays a mean trumpet.

Percy is a tall overweight bear of a man and is dressed in a dark suit and wears glasses, also dark African American, also late twenties. He always has a troubled look on his face. When he plays, he stoops over the keyboard of the piano with his eyes nearly touching the keys.

The crowd goes wild with applause as the set finishes.

Percy and Lincoln go up to the bar.

PERCY

That's it man! You've nailed it, brother!

LINCOLN

Pretty cool all right!

Lincoln leans on the bar and speaks to the bar tender.

LINCOLN (cont'd)

Hey Mac, how about a drink for the working man?

BAR TENDER

Look Percy you know the rules. I'll lose my job, man!

LINCOLN

One drink?

BAR TENDER

No can do! You guys were hot tonight!

LINCOLN

Yeh right!

PERCY

Let's get out of here Linc before the trouble comes.

LINCOLN

(getting angry)
All I want is one lousy drink.

PERCY

Come on man let's go!

A big gangster type man comes up to the boys.

GANGSTER
You got a problem?

LINCOLN
I want a drink is all.

PERCY
Not again, man! Let's get out while we can.

GANGSTER
Good advice. Take it and scram!

LINCOLN
What if I don't want to?

*The gangster pulls out a revolver and shoots Percy and
Lincoln dead, without another word spoken.*

Smokey haze fills the screen. Credits appear.

---

2.   **INT. WILL'S KITCHEN AREA**

*It's now 2012 in the small country Australian town of
Ballinga.*

*Will Martin, the drummer, is phoning his band to get them
to a rehearsal.*

*Will is around thirty five with short neat brown hair,
smallish in size and build, strong bicep muscles that bulge
from the T shirts he loves to wear.*

WILL
(on the phone)
Mike, listen to me will you ... if we could only rehearse a bit more ... OK,
fair enough mate, see you then.

Will's wife EMMA wanders in.

*EMMA is also around thirty five, a big boned woman, taller
than Will, carrying a bit extra weight, striking long red hair,
casual dress.*

EMMA

How's it going love?

WILL
They don't get it! How shit do we have to get before even the pub won't
hire us!

EMMA
(smiling)
Now who else have they got to choose from.

WILL
(frowning)
That's just what they think too! Nobody will ever take me seriously, is all!

EMMA

We're farmers love, not mainstream musos.

WILL

It's not good enough! It's not what I planned!

EMMA

It'll all work out for the best.

WILL

(frustrated)

Sure.

3.   INT. LOCAL BAR

The band is playing as badly as ever on the usual set of songs. Some of the drinkers even cringe at the crappy playing.

One of the locals, Ernie, jokes with the hotel owner.

Ernie is a big man, mid-forties, well over six feet, the local mechanic, his hands are rough with dirty fingernails, longish dark curly hair, dressed in clean jeans and a clean checked shirt.

ERNIE

I reckon my dog could play better than this mob.

Everyone laughs and John, the owner shrugs his shoulders in despair.

John is also a big man, mid-fifties, very kind roundish face, greying hair, dressed in casual pants and a short sleeved shirt.

JOHN

They are a bit rough.

ERNIE

It's putting me off me beer!

Everyone laughs again.

JOHN

I don't reckon anything could do that mate!

More laughter. The set finishes and John goes around the bar.

JOHN (cont'd)

I'll have a word with them.

John goes over to the band as they are packing up their gear.

JOHN (cont'd)

Can I have a word, Will?

WILL

Sure John, what's up?

*John takes Will out of earshot of the rest of the band and
the onlooking drinkers.*

JOHN

Mate, it's a bit amateur night out with you guys, if you get my drift.

WILL

Hey mate, don't sack us just yet. I know we can do better.

JOHN

I've been pretty fair with you, you know that!

WILL

(pleading)

If we don't improve by next Saturday, I'll pull the pin myself! Can you live
with that?

John looks Will squarely in the eyes and smiles.

JOHN

I guess one more week won't hurt too much.

John walks back to the bar.

WILL

Thanks mate!

*Will goes back to the four other band members, Chloe, the
singer, looks up as he comes into view.*

*Chloe is around thirty, five feet seven inches tall, dyed blond
hair, sort of tarty looking with skin tight leather pants and
a revealing silk shirt.*

CHLOE

What was that all about?

WILL

Sacking us!

CHLOE

The bastard.

Mike, the pianist, picks up on this and moves closer.
*Mike is a big man, farmer, around thirty five, wears old
jeans, short sleeved shirt and runners. Longish blond hair.*

MIKE

I guess we do sound a bit shit!

CHLOE

Speak for yourself! If you must know, you're the biggest shit around here!

MIKE

Whatever, princess.

Don is around forty, average height and complexion, very content to slip under the radar with what he wears and says.

DON
(calmly)
Do we get another shot at it, or are we completely done?

WILL
Actually he's agreed to let us do the gig one more time next Saturday night ... then it's over.

DON
Ok then! Why don't we have a real good rehearsal on Wednesday night at Mike's place and see what happens!

WILL
I've been trying to get you guys to do that for the past three months!

MIKE
Ok let's do that then.

CHLOE
Alright. I'll be there!

Bob, the bass player, sticks his hand up.

Bob is a tall wiry sort of guy, late twenties, always wears way out colours on his pants and shirts, cream pointy shoes. He wears his hair like Elvis and has a chain around his neck. He has an assortment of tattoos.

BOB
Sounds good to me!

WILL
Alright guys, this is it! We can concentrate on some of the late thirties jazz numbers and go out in style!

A juke box starts to belt out a rock tune as the band start packing their gear away.

In the background, two translucent figures are seen - they are the spirits of Percy and Lincoln.

PERCY
I reckon these boys need a bit of help.

LINCOLN
Are you talking about the one year deal the big man told us about?

PERCY
Could be worse?

LINCOLN
(laughing)
Not much worse, man!

PERCY

Let's give them a taste of real music.

Percy goes straight for Mike and as the lights flicker, enters him.

Lincoln goes over to Don and enters him.

Mike and Don both startle.

MIKE

Did it suddenly get cold in here?

DON

Thought the same thing meself.

The other members of the band look strangely at Don and Mike and keep packing their gear away.

4. INT. MIKE'S HOUSE

A few of the guys are in the house setting up the drums and amps.

Chloe comes in through the open door.

CHLOE

Hi guys!

Will stops what he is doing and smiles at her.

WILL

Hey CHLOE we're nearly ready to go.

CHLOE

Great!

Chloe unpacks a mike from her handbag and fits it onto the mike-stand.

Bob and Don are heavy into a conversation in the corner of the room.

BOB

... you were right about the cost of fertilizer going up. I'm not sure we can keep juggling the books.

DON

Yeh, it's tough alright. Will's been muck spreading from his pig dung.

BOB

Yeah?

DON

Ask him about it later.

BOB

I will! Thanks!

Mike taps out a few notes on the piano and everyone looks up at him.

MIKE

I can make a coffee if anyone wants one.

CHLOE

(smirking)

Jess left you again?

MIKE

Yep! Two weeks back, I guess she'd really had enough this time.

CHLOE

Surprised she lasted six months!

WILL

Cut it out you two, we need to practise.

Will hands out some music scores to the guys.

WILL (cont'd)

Don found it on the web.

MIKE

Looks good, let's give it a bash!

Will taps out a time on his drums and they all start playing their parts.

Mike stops playing suddenly and turns to Bob.

MIKE (cont'd)

I think you should wait a few bars before you come in.

BOB

Where do you reckon?

They both look at the music score.

MIKE

About here I think.

BOB

Ok!

MIKE

Sort of run your hand down the fretboard and do some sort of slap on the notes.

BOB

I can't do that!

DON

It's not that hard, Bob. Here I'll show you.

Don puts his trumpet down and picks up the bass guitar.
Does a slick slide and starts slapping gently on the strings.

DON (cont'd)

See what I mean?

BOB
Gee! That's not too bad!

DON
Stay loose, don't strangle it.

BOB
Like this?

DON
(smiling)
Spot on.

BOB
Thanks!

Will starts tapping again and the band begins to play.
Chloe sings and the songs sounds pretty cool.

WILL
(beaming)
That's what I've been talking about guys!

MIKE
Will, you're coming in with a heavy off beat after each roll. Be better if you switched to brushes to give some variation.

WILL
I can try that.

CHLOE
What about me Mr Smartypants?

MIKE
No! You nailed it!

Chloe blushes a bit as she acknowledges the grins from the other guys.

CHLOE
Let's do it again! I reckon I can do even better!

They all laugh.

WILL
Sounds like a plan!

At the end of the rehearsal Bob chats to Don quietly.

BOB
I never knew you played a bit of bass?

DON
A long time back I tinkered with it. Good session eh?

BOB
And you're doing something different with that horn of yours as well.

DON

What do you mean?

BOB

Sounds real American!

They both burst out laughing.

WILL

A special session guys! See you at six thirty Saturday!

5.   INT. ERNIE'S GARAGE

The clock has just clicked over to twelve thirty as Ernie comes up for a breather under the hood of a shiny Mercedes.

ERNIE

It's the head alright!

A well-dressed man accompanied by two attractive women gets closer to Ernie.

Ben is average height, late fifties, bald, very smart casual outfit, has a gold chain around his neck and rings on his fingers. He looks wealthy.

BEN

Fixable?

ERNIE

Yeah, but not today, mate!

BEN

(a bit frustrated)
I have to be in Melbourne lunchtime Monday...

ERNIE

Not in this car!

BEN

You are kidding me!

ERNIE

It's bloody Saturday and I'll have to hoist the damn thing ... Nah, I promised me kids to take them fishing this arvo. No can do!

BEN

What about tomorrow?

ERNIE

I promised the wife to do some gardening around the house...

BEN

Gardening?

ERNIE

Yeah!

BEN
How much will the job cost me anyway?

ERNIE
I reckon it will set you back around eight hundred bucks, give or take.

The two girls start to get a bit restless.

Suzy is in her early twenties, long blond hair, trim and tall, wearing tight jeans and Rolling Stones T shirt.

SUZY
Are we stuck here then?

BEN
Pretty much!

SUZY
What's there to do on Saturday night here?

ERNIE
(laughing gently)
There's the pub. And there's the pub!

BEN
Look mate, what if I was to pay you fifteen hundred dollars for you to get me going tomorrow?

ERNIE
I don't know!

Ernie goes off and thinks for a bit and then faces Ben again.

ERNIE (cont'd)
I'll call the wife.

BEN
(relieved)
Thanks mate!

Ernie goes inside his office. Pretends to call. Comes back outside.

ERNIE
It's a done deal!

BEN
Brilliant! Where is the pub anyway?

ERNIE
Can't miss it! Only tall building in town!

Ben grabs some bags and a briefcase. Beckons to the two girls.

BEN
Come on! We're spending the night!

SUZY

(facetiously)
Great!

BEN

(looking back at Ernie)
I'll see you tomorrow then?

ERNIE

Should be done by about two thirty or there abouts.

BEN

(waving)
Fair enough! Thanks again!

Ben, Suzy and Belinda trudge down the dusty road into the main street of the town.

Belinda is late twenties, blond, more conservative in her appearance, smaller than Suzy, wearing a longish dress with a sweater draped over her shoulders.

BELINDA

(really annoyed)
You have got to be joking!

BEN

It's only one night. Treat it as an experiment of where not to end up in.

SUZY

Sure!

BELINDA

Oh my God! Is that the hotel?

The only building of any size comes into view and it is not in the best condition.

People are starting to drop into the pub for lunch as Ben makes his way to the office.

Ben rings the counter bell and waits. Pretty soon John turns up.

JOHN

G'day!

BEN

G'day mate! Do you have a couple of rooms for the night?

JOHN

I reckon we can fit you in. Not much happening around here.

BEN

Car's being fixed at the garage.

JOHN

Ernie's a good mechanic, used to work for John Deere, you're in good hands.

                              BEN
                      That's good to know.

                              JOHN
              Just sign the register and I'll get you settled in.

                              BEN
              Thanks! Any decent places to eat in town?

                              JOHN
              Pub's it I'm afraid. It's not bad though!

Ben looks at the girls and signs the register.

                              BEN
                           Visa Ok?

                              JOHN
                            Yep!

                              BEN
                      Thank God for that!

| 6. | **INT. HOTEL DINING ROOM** | **LUNCHTIME** |

*Ben and the girls are enjoying burgers with chips. The girls
are having a glass of white wine and Ben is having a beer.*

*A poster is seen by Ben stating "Where There's a Will,
tonight 7:30!"*

Ben points to it.

                              BEN
                 Whatever it is… It's only one night!

The girls look at each other in a bored out fashion.

| 7. | **INT. HOTEL DINING ROOM** | **EVENING** |

*Ben and the girls are enjoying a hearty meal of steaks and
pasta. There is a bottle of red wine on the table.*

Will and Emma are seen having a quiet meal together.

*The room feels suddenly crowded there are about sixty
people milling around.*

*Ben notices Ernie at the bar drinking a beer and goes over
to him.*

                              BEN
                       Catch any fish?

It takes a while for Ernie to recognise Ben.

                              ERNIE
                     Oh G'day! Yeah, we
                      caught a couple.

BEN

That's good.

ERNIE

(smirking)

You're in for a treat with Will tonight.

Ernie points to the stage where the band is starting to get organised.

BEN

Ok are they?

ERNIE

(laughing)

Pretty terrible if you ask me.

BEN

Oh well, whatever! See you tomorrow!

Ernie goes back to his beer still chuckling to himself.

Ben goes back to his table as Will takes the microphone to the centre of the stage.

WILL

This will be our last show.

A few claps and jeers resound through the room.

WILL (cont'd)

My thanks to John for putting up with us for this long.

More laughs and applause.

WILL (cont'd)

We'll start with a new song from us and an oldie from the vaults. Hope you like it.

EMMA

(yelling out)

You show 'em Will!

Will goes back behind the drum kit and waits till the chatter dies down a bit.

Will winks at Mike who starts into the new song.

Almost immediately the crowd pick up on the new vibe and quality of the playing.

Even Ernie has started to take some interest.

Mike glances over at Will, who quickly switches to brushes, and smiles back, mouthing "sorry mate."

Don's solo takes everyone by surprise. Will has sweat running down his face.

The song finishes, Chloe sings the last lyric, and the crowd is still in shock.

Ben starts clapping and pretty soon everyone is cheering.

BEN

(to the girls)

What do you make of that?

SUZY

Bloody brilliant!

BEN

(nodding)

Aha!

Ben catches Ernie's eye and he shrugs his shoulders in disbelief.

Will wipes his face and in a whisper announces the next song.

WILL

Hope you like this one too.

One song after another is delivered like nothing this crowd had heard before in style and quality, the applause is nothing the band has heard before either.

During the break, Ben holds his hand up to John who comes over to the table.

BEN

They're not half bad.

JOHN

Tonight is different alright.

BEN

Buy them all a drink on my tab if you wouldn't mind and ask the drummer to come have a chat.

JOHN

Sure thing!

John walks off and the girls look over at Ben.

BELINDA

(cynically)

What's on that mind of yours?

JOHN

(smiling)

Oh nothing much, just thought they might like a few gigs in Melbourne is all.

We see John chatting to the band and pointing over at Ben's table.

Will walks over, sweat dripping from his brow. He wipes it off.

WILL

Hi guys, glad you're liking our show. Thanks for the drinks too!

BEN
(shaking Will's hand)
Take a seat! I'm a promoter and your sound has me intrigued.

WILL
Yeah?

BEN
I haven't heard that sort of arrangement and playing for a long time.

WILL
Are you kidding me. We have been sacked, this is our last gig!

BEN
Straight up! Are you interested in doing three gigs in Melbourne next
Friday and Saturday night?

BELINDA
(smiling)
You guys were really hot out there!

WILL
I don't know. We're farmers you see.

Ben
How does a thousand dollars a gig sound?

WILL
(calculating in his head)
You mean six hundred each for the three gigs?

BEN
(laughing)
No! I mean three thousand a head!

Will is a bit taken aback.

WILL
I could sure use the money right now.

BEN
Why don't you chat with the other boys and let me know after your next
set.

WILL
I can do that!

John brings Will his drink as Will gets up to leave the table.

JOHN
Get this into you, you are hot tonight!

WILL
Thanks John, I'm hearing that a bit.

BEN
Catch you later?

WILL

One way or the other!

Will waltzes back to the band as Emma falls in along side.

EMMA

What was that all about, hon?

By this time the other band members mill around Will as well.

WILL

Three gigs in Melbourne next weekend. Three thousand each!

EMMA

Wow!

WILL

Let's do this show and chat it out after! Ok?

There is a general mutter of approval between the band members and they quickly get on with the show.

---

8.   **INT. TELSTRA DOME**

Ben is discussing logistics with Will as the others perform sound checks.

Emma and Bob are close by watching Will intently.

BEN

Your gig starts at around eight thirty.

WILL

Tomorrow night too?

BEN

Yeah! There is also a late spot at Bennett's Lane.

WILL

(faking it)

Cool!

BEN

Now listen carefully, I want you to start with that track you opened with last Saturday and then the two songs I emailed you.

WILL

Sure! We rehearsed those tracks, pretty cool sound too.

BEN

Good! There's some people listening to you and who knows what will happen if we play our cards right.

WILL

I got it, first three songs.

BEN

After that you can play whatever. I'll give you the signal when your gig time is up, I'd say about forty minutes.

WILL

Too easy! Thanks again Ben!

Bob smiles awkwardly at Emma. They seem a bit overwhelmed by where they are.

BOB

I'm sure glad the cars are back at the hotel. This city driving's not for me.

EMMA

Hang in there. Just go with the flow.

BOB

I'm trying! Bloody nervous, is all.

Emma smiles affectionately at Bob and then goes over to Will.

The stadium is suddenly filling with people. Some big posters about a top French band are also seen around the place.

Ben signals to Will to get ready for the curtain to go up as a young man, Walter, mid-twenties, blond hair, in a conservative suit, walks to the centre stage.

WALTER

(on the microphone to the audience)
Let's give a big hand to these here local boys, Where There's a Will!

A few isolated claps, and the chatter can still be heard as a low hum.

The curtain goes up and Will taps his drum sticks a couple of times, winks at Emma, the band starts playing.

Soon the audience is deadly quiet, listening intently. When the song finishes there is a wild applause and whistling.

WILL

(a bit flushed)
Thanks guys, it's our first gig in Melbourne.

More applause and whistles.

WILL (cont'd)

Hope you enjoy the rest of the show.

Will looks over at Mike, who starts a few chords on the piano and the next song starts.

Chloe starts humming a few bars of the intro and then breaks out in full voice.

More applause and cheering. We see the French band watching from the wings and looking mighty impressed.

WILL (cont'd)

Let me introduce the band members. Chloe on vocals.

More applause.

WILL (cont'd)

Mike on the keyboard.

More applause. Mike plays a few extra chords on the piano to the delight of the now growing crowd.

WILL (cont'd)

Don on trumpet.

More applause.

WILL (cont'd)

Bob on bass and my name is Will.

More applause and whistles as Mike starts in on the next song.
Ben and Suzy are seen chatting with a couple of people at a table near the front of the band.
Ben winks at Will and smiles.
One song after another go down to much applause and soon it is time for Ben to indicate to Will that it's one last song to go.

WILL (cont'd)

Thanks guys, you've been great to play to tonight ... we have another gig to go to so this will be our final song. Coming up after us are the fantastic Miller's Bluesmen. Thanks again!

Music from the gig overlaps and links every scene where the music has been playing and the scene changes. This should not be the ONLY means or technique used.

---

9.   **INT. TAXI CAB WITH WILL, EMMA AND BEN**

Will and Emma are cuddled up on the back with Ben in the front seat. The car is driving through the city area.

BEN

(looking back at Will)

Not bad for a first gig in the big smoke.

WILL

(a bit overwhelmed by it all)

We really appreciate the opportunity.

BEN

You guys are great! It's a style that we haven't heard for a long time.

EMMA

See babe, I knew you could do it!

WILL

It's like a dream.

Ben

(more serious)

If you want the dream to continue and if you'd like me to manage your career, then I'm available.

WILL

You kidding! Where do I sign?

BEN

Talk it over with the others and we can all chat it through over breakfast tomorrow. It has to be all of you or none of you.

WILL

Sounds OK to me.

Ben turns away from them as he faces the traffic and immediately starts up on his mobile phone.

Will and Emma kiss each other.

10.   **INT. ANOTHER TAXI CAB**

Don is rummaging through a stack of old papers. Mike is deep in thought. The car is racing through the city, following the other two cabs.

MIKE

You know Don it's a bit weird ...

DON

What is?

MIKE

One minute we are struggling to pay the rent and the music's crap. Next minute it's like a huge turnaround.

Mike gazes out at the traffic.

MIKE (cont'd)

It's weird mate!

DON

Yeah I guess you could say that.

Changing the subject.

DON (cont'd)

Take a look at this old song, tell me what you think.

Don hands over a crumbled piece of paper to Mike and immediately he is humming the tune and tapping out a beat.

DON (cont'd)

Not bad, eh?

MIKE

Pretty interesting! Where'd you find it?

DON

Oh, I've had it for years and for some reason brought it with me. Worth a try wouldn't you say?

Mike looks cautiously back at Don

MIKE

You think Chloe can handle it?

DON

Worth a go.

Suzy is in the front seat of the cab and overhears the conversation. She appears keen on Mike.

SUZY

It hums pretty cool …

MIKE

Forgot you were there …

SUZY

Don't do that Mike. I was hoping we could get a drink together later.

MIKE

(looking mighty interested)
Sounds like a good idea to me.

SUZY

Its a plan then!

A few knowing glances pass between them.

11.   INT. BENNETT'S LANE

The cabs pull up outside Bennett's Lane and the band and entourage are ushered up to the players' dressing room. Some great jazz is being played and the guys are a little in awe of the quality they will have to follow.

BEN

(sensing the nervousness)
They sound pretty good...

WILL

Sure do!

BEN

Well let me tell you something! You guys sound even better!

Silent disbelief in the band's eyes.

SUZY

You guys are bloody brilliant!

BEN

It's good to be modest. Just do the same set as before and you'll knock them dead!

Will and Emma burst out laughing and the tension is eased.

Pretty soon they are on the stage getting the feel of things. The audience has crowded the bar and not really taking much notice of the band.

Chloe screws her mike into the stand and taps it. A few people notice the booming sound but quickly go back to their conversations.

There is no introduction as Will taps his drum stick a few times and the music begins.

Like the previous show, the crowd is somewhat awe-struck and highly appreciative of the performance.

12. **INT. CITY HOTEL BREAKFAST ROOM**	**NEXT MORNING**

Mike and Suzy wander in and join the group. Ben does not appear happy seeing Suzy like that, but tries to not let it show. Emma notices it and smiles at Ben.

EMMA

(to Mike)

Big night!

Mike looks a little flushed.

MIKE

Got it in one!

Mike smiles at Suzy and pours a cup of coffee for them both.

MIKE (cont'd)

What's good around here?

BOB

Everything mate!

A few meaningful looks surround Mike & Suzy as they start hoeing into their breakfast.

Mike catches everyone looking at him and exclaims.

MIKE

What?

WILL

It's all good Mike. Ben wants to talk about the next gig tonight and the band's future as far as he's concerned.

Will looks over at Ben and winks.

WILL (cont'd)

Over to you mate. We are all ears.

Ben gives Mike and Suzy another dirty look.

BEN

Two good shows guys. Tonight should be just a repeat.

Ben pauses and looks around at the eager faces watching him.

BEN (cont'd)

I'm liking what I'm hearing and with a little tweaking, you guys could cash in big time.

EMMA

Do you really think so?

BEN

I do. I'm prepared, if you want to go the distance with me, to sign you up and take you all on the ride of your lives.

DON

We are farmers, mate. What about our farms?

CHLOE

Yeah but Don, isn't this what you've always talked about?

DON

It is, but it's all happening too quick for my liking.

WILL

What about our farms, Ben? Sure, we have the passion for the music, but the farms are everything to us.

Ben looks Will in the eye very seriously.

BEN

How much do you owe the bank so that you don't go under?

Will looks very flushed and gazes over at Emma.

EMMA

I didn't say anything, hon!

BEN

And you Don ... I understand the bank's been knocking on your door too!

DON

(angrily)

Who have you been yabbing to! None of your bloody business!

BEN

It could be my business! I can make all those dramas disappear in the shake of a pen on a contract. Bank taken care of, your farms with managers on them when you're not there...

DON

What if I don't want your bloody help!

BEN

That's OK too. We do tonight's gig, you each get your three grand and that will be that. No hard feelings. I'd be disappointed but will respect whatever decision you come to ... I mean that.

Everyone goes silent for a deafening minute.

Suzy drops her coffee mug onto the floor and everyone bursts out laughing.

SUZY

Sorry! I'm all fingers right now.

Suzy glances over at Mike and mouths "sorry" to him and he smiles back at her.

Will gets up and looks nervously at the table.

WILL

Shit! I never thought we could ever get an offer like that! Mike, what do you think?

MIKE

It's a game changer all right! I'm up for it!

WILL

Don?

DON

Not sure Will. I don't know!

BEN

Take your time, it's a big decision.

CHLOE

I'm in! Wow!

Bob

If Don agrees, I'll do it...

DON

(smiling)

Pressure's on me then.

WILL

It's all of us or none of us!

CHLOE

Come on Don!

DON

OK I'll give it a burl!

A lot of smiles all round. Ben pulls a contract from his briefcase and hands it to Will.

BEN

Read it and get everyone to sign. It's going to be unreal!

Will carefully reads the contract, hands it to Emma.

WILL

It looks OK to me.

Emma takes her time to read the fine print and seems satisfied.

EMMA

I'd say sign before he wakes up!

Everyone laughs. Will signs first and hands it around the table. Don is the last to sign.

DON

I guess we've done it now!

BEN

(signing his name too)
Yep! We are in for the long haul!

---

13.   INT. KITCHEN AT WILL'S FARM   **EARLY MORNING**

Will, deep in thought, and wearing his old Stubbies shorts, stares out at one of the paddocks from the kitchen window. Emma, still half asleep, wanders into the room in a nightie, pops the kettle on and then notices Will.

EMMA

(softly)
Hi hon. couldn't sleep?

Will takes his time to release his gaze on the farm. He slowly faces Emma. He looks a bit worn out and stressed.

EMMA (cont'd)

Worried about our farm?

WILL

It's like a catch 22. If we went on the same way we've been going, we would have lost it! I mean, I would have lost it!

EMMA

We would have lost it, hon.

WILL

Yeah right! Now I have to walk away from it, to save it …

EMMA

You did it, hon! If it wasn't for you we would be up to our necks in a drama. It would have been terrible!

WILL

I love this farm!

EMMA

I know you do. So do I!

WILL

Someone else moving in and running things. It doesn't feel right!

EMMA

(putting her arms around Will)

It's not forever!

*The kettle starts to whistle and Emma goes and makes a
cup of tea for them both.*

EMMA (cont'd)

Toast, hon?

Will nods back.

EMMA (cont'd)

When's the manager guy arriving?

WILL

Tomorrow I guess. We fly out the next day, so I guess he'll bunk down on
the couch tomorrow night and that will be that.

*They both share a meaningful look and a relieving smile
as well.*

EMMA

LA and Chicago for two months! I never dreamed of going to those places!

WILL

Me neither.

14.   INT. MELBOURNE INTERNATIONAL AIRPORT

*Everyone in the band is there. Belinda has a stack of
passports in her briefcase and is checking the right ones
go to the correct person.*

BELINDA

(to Bob)

Here's your passport Bob and make sure you hold onto it!

BOB

You're a gem, Bel'! What would we do without you?

BELINDA

(sarcastically)

Probably leave without your guitar. Something like that!

BOB

Not bloody likely! My baby is the first thing on my mind ... always!

BELINDA

Well! I guess that counts me out then, doesn't it?

*Bob looks gingerly back at Belinda as if he had missed a
sexual opportunity. She smiles knowingly back.*

Will and Emma are busy repacking their on-board luggage.

101

Mike and Suzy are giving each other some deep and meaningful looks.

15.   INT. L.A. AIRPORT

A sign says "Welcome to Los Angeles". There are long queues at customs.

BEN
Better get used to it!

EMMA
Is it always like this?

BEN
Pretty much. Stay cool.

WILL
(grimacing)
That's why I love my farm!

Emma looks lovingly back at Will.

16.   INT. REHEARSAL STUDIO   LATER THAT DAY

Percy and Lincoln are seen translucently hovering in the background.

LINCOLN
At least we are back in The States at last!

PERCY
It aint Chicago, Linc. We aint home yet!

LINCOLN
Yeah! Yeah! In three weeks we will be. What then?

PERCY
(a little agitated)
What then! Revenge brother! That's what!

LINCOLN
(resignedly)
That was seventy years ago ...

Percy looks a little shocked by the thought of all that time that had passed

PERCY
(angrily)
I don't care! I got to do something!

The band is jamming an old melody and the spirits leave their conversation and sort of jam along.

Don is really letting loose with the horn and attracting a lot of attention from a group of onlookers, who are reacting as if they had never heard a trumpet being played that way.

At the end of the song there is a wild applause. The band, as a whole, look a bit embarrassed... But not Ben who is smiling inwardly as if he knew it all the time.

17.   INT. L.A. NIGHTCLUB

The band is in full swing and being very much appreciated.

WILL
(into the mike)
Last song I'm afraid ... we are heading to Chicago later on this morning ... Here is a track that Mike, our keyboard player, has written. It's called "My farm back home".

The audience applauds and whistles. Mike starts into the track as the band joins in.

Emma is seen off stage with a tear in her eye, lost in thought.

The song finishes to more applause and the guys grab their gear and race off to waiting taxis.

18.   INT. CHICAGO AIRPORT

All the Australians look tired. The spirits seem excited.

LINCOLN
(singing in a whisper)
Sweet home Chicago, man. Finally!

PERCY
Yeah!

The spirits look at each other.

PERCY (cont'd)
You be cool, man! This is someone else's journey! Know what I mean?

LINCOLN
Yeah man! I'll be cool!

Bob is seen holding Belinda's hand as well as his Bass Guitar in his other hand.

BELINDA
(looking at the guitar)
I never figured my competition would be a guitar!

BOB
It's a long story Bell' ...

BELINDA
I'd love to hear it some time.

BOB
You will ... it's all good.

*They share an awkward kiss. Ben sees everything and is a
bit concerned.*

*Mike and Don are walking together looking at old photos
on the wall.*

MIKE
Hey mate, it's a bit weird, but I was getting this feeling that I already know
this place.

DON
Deja Vu I guess! The same thought crossed my mind too!

MIKE
I reckon I'm bloody tired! It's been a heck of a schedule!

DON
Yeah! Who'd have picked it?

Suzy catches them up and slings an arm around Mike.

SUZY
You don't lose me that quick!

DON
I'm out of here mate!

Don walks over to Ben & Will & Emma.

SUZY
(to Don)
Don't go because of me!

Don shoots her a nice smile and keeps walking.

MIKE
He's OK! He's a smart cookie alright!

They embrace and kiss, as CHLOE passes them by.

CHLOE
Come on, young lovers!

MIKE
Sounds like a song title.

CHLOE
(a little annoyed)
I got to get to that hotel. I'm stuffed!

Chloe walks off and Mike and Suzy just burst out in laughter.

---

19.   INT. CHICAGO BLUES BAR

*Ben is showing the band the club and giving a bit of a
history on the players that had been there.*

BEN

All the greats, at one time or another have played here.

Don and Mike are looking a bit strange as they gaze at the old photographs on the wall.

The two spirits are also quite excited as well.

LINCOLN

This is the place alright!

PERCY

Sure changed a lot ... But you're right! We copped it right over there where the bar used to be.

LINCOLN

(a bit contemplative)

I know it was my fault, that night. Sorry Perc, what a life we could have had

...

PERCY

Yeah! I wonder what happened to my people, is all!

LINCOLN

Maybe we can find out?

Don and Mike sit on a bar stool and look at each other.

DON

I've got that feeling again!

MIKE

Me too!

DON

Crazy crazy, is all I can say!

Mike wanders over to a barman and quite surprisingly asks him a question.

MIKE

Hey man, did somebody get killed here ... A long time back?

The barman, who has a perpetual smile on his face looks long and hard at Mike.

BAR TENDER

You part of the Australian combo playing here tonight?

MIKE

Yeah! That's right!

The two men share a look at each other.

MIKE (cont'd)

Something did happen here, didn't it?

BAR TENDER

Well, it was just after the war, so I'm told, this place was run by the mob.

*Don also wanders over to the bar as Suzy and Belinda
make their way as well.*

BAR TENDER (cont'd)
Not much to tell, but two of the musicians got into a fight with one of the
owners and they ended up dead.

BELINDA
What happened then?

BAR TENDER
The bodies were dumped in the river and life went back to normal.

BELINDA
Wow!

BAR TENDER
You have to understand how it was back then. No-one said anything about
anything! If you get my drift.

DON
What about the families of the murdered musos?

BAR TENDER
Can't say! Before my time!

DON
So who would know? I'm interested?

BAR TENDER
Well, there's an old timer, Jack Henderson, haven't seen him for ages, used
to work here. He might know … He's certainly old enough!

The bar tender chuckles a bit to himself.

MIKE
So where does this Jack Henderson live now?

BAR TENDER
Old age home I guess! Don't rightly know!

Ben marches over and taps Mike on the shoulder.

BEN
Mike, I want you to check out the old grand piano, so there are no
surprises tonight.

MIKE
Sure Ben!

The group marches away towards the stage area.
The bar tender has a confused look on his face.

---

20.   INT. CHICAGO BLUES BAR   NIGHT - FOUR WEEKS LATER

The band is in full swing to a highly appreciative audience.
Ben is seen chatting with a group of business type people.

*The gig finishes around four in the morning and the crowd
wanders off.*

*The band is having a few drinks in the players' lounge area
and everyone is on the point of hyped up exhaustion.*

BEN

That was spot on guys!

WILL

Thanks mate! Got to hit that sack!

BEN

You will! First I have to tell you there were some label guys here tonight
and they are talking a record deal! What do you say to that?

The room goes very quiet for a time as the words sink in.

CHLOE

(excitedly)
You for real!

Ben winks at her and nods.

CHLOE (cont'd)

To record here or home?

BEN

Hasn't been worked out, but I'd assume here at their studio. Maybe in LA,
they have a studio there too!

CHLOE

I don't know about you, but I'm a bit over the hotel and traveling scene.
Really looking forward to going home. This has been loads of fun but very
gruelling!

BEN

You guys are on a roll! Strike while you can, I say, but it's your call and we
can discuss it when we're not so tired if you wish?

WILL

That's a great idea. Chloe, I miss my farm too! Bloody too tired to think
straight!

BOB

Yeah! Let's get back to the hotel and catch up later in the day. There's no
gig tomorrow is there?

BEN

That's right! How about lunch by the river at say one O'clock?

*Everyone mumbles agreement and as they are all departing
for the hotel, the bar tender comes over to Don.*

BAR TENDER

Excuse me ... were you the guy asking about old Jack Henderson a while
back?

DON
(suddenly interested)
Why yes! Has he been in?

BAR TENDER
I haven't seen him, but a friend of his was in tonight and told me he was in
a bad way at the Mercy of God Hospice.

By this time Mike and Suzy wander over and join in.

MIKE
Is that close by?

BAR TENDER
I think it's on Main Street but any cab driver worth his salt will know it.

DON
Thanks mate! It could be interesting to chat with him if he's up to it.

BAR TENDER
You're welcome! Say, you guys are very good you know! I've heard a lot
going through this club and it's been a refreshing pleasure to listen to you
guys!

MIKE
Thanks mate! Appreciate it!

Belinda wanders over as the bar tender wanders off.

BELINDA
What was that about?

DON
Another fan!

Everyone shares a laugh.

DON (cont'd)
He told us about an old timer he thought we might like to chat with. Very
nice of him too!

Mike whispers in Don's ear.

MIKE
I reckon we should check it out tomorrow when we get up.

DON
What about the lunch meeting?

MIKE
Maybe we can do both.

DON
Sounds good to me, then.

MIKE
Cool!

Mike and Don are taking a taxi going across town.

Ben is on the phone.

Will and Emma are curled up in bed asleep.

22.   **INT. MERCY OF GOD HOSPICE**

Mike and Don go inside the hospice and make straight for the front desk. There is a lot of people milling around.

MIKE
(to the nurse on the desk)
We are friends of Jack Henderson, can you direct me to his room?

NURSE
(looking a bit surprised)
He doesn't get too many visitors. Friends you say?

MIKE
Sort of friends of friends. How is he doing today?

NURSE
He had a bad night, you know. He's ninety eight years old and I'd say he won't see another year through.

MIKE
Oh! That's too bad!

NURSE
I'll check for you.

The nurse picks up the phone and speaks into it for a few seconds.

NURSE (cont'd)
He's actually having his lunch if you want to go see him. Second floor, room two one three.

MIKE
Thanks we'll take a look in on him then.

Mike and Don briskly walk up two flights of stairs and without too much difficulty find the ward.

There are six patients in the room, all having a bite to eat.

Don goes over to the closest bed to enquire.

DON
Would you be Jack Henderson by any chance?

The man goes on with his eating but points to a bed by the window.

DON (cont'd)
(already heading in that direction)
Thanks!

Mike joins Don as they reach Jack's bed. He is looking quite frail, but is alert enough and also having his lunch.

MIKE
(to Jack)
Looks tasty enough!

JACK
(somewhat startled)
Who are you fellas?

MIKE
Just musicians from down under, playing at the club you used to work at...

JACK
I'm not well you know!

DON
I'm Don and this Mike! Do you mind having a chat with us about the old days?

JACK
Why not! I don't know much though!

Mike and Don pull up chairs near Jack's bed.

The spirits of Percy & Lincoln are seen hovering around the bed as well.

PERCY
I know this dude, I'm sure of it!

LINCOLN
Yeah! He was there that night all right!

PERCY
He didn't pull no trigger...

LINCOLN
I know! He was just the sweeper! I remember him!

Jack finishes his food and a nurse props him up a bit higher in the bed.

JACK
(to the nurse as she is leaving)
Thanks!

Jack focusses his attention on Mike and Don and seems a little uneasy.

JACK (cont'd)

What was it you wanted to know?

Mike and Don look at each other and then both gaze intently at Jack ... it unsettles him a bit.

JACK (cont'd)

Hey! What's your game?

DON

(smiling now)

I guess it's all about the shooting that took place after the war...

JACK

(tense)

That wasn't me...

DON

I know! You were there though!

Silence in the room and there is fear in Jack's eyes.

DON (cont'd)

Those two boys had families and friends. I just want to know what happened after you dumped the bodies....

JACK

How the fuck do you guys know anything about that? I never told anyone

...

MIKE

You mean, where you dumped them and what happened after that?

JACK

(emotionally)

I think about that night every day of my god-damned life!

MIKE

Chicago River?

JACK

Actually no! Joe had a building going up... Where "The Loop" is now... Dumped and cemented... It was horrible...

DON

No police action, friends come looking for them?

Jack looks them squarely in the eyes

JACK

They were black, no-one did nothing!

Don and Mike look a little shocked.

JACK (cont'd)

I don't know why I'm telling you this stuff for.

DON

Closure and peace of mind.

Jack nods wisely acknowledging the gravity of the words.

JACK

There was this one woman who came in a couple of times asking about one of them ... Can't remember her name or which one she was asking about.

DON

What did you tell her?

JACK

Nothing! She was pregnant too, I do remember that. A pretty young thing she was. I sure felt awful sorry about her, but it was what it was and I couldn't say anything. You know what I mean?

Don and Mike, and the spirits of Percy and Lincoln, look very saddened by this news.

PERCY

That's my Lucy!

JACK

I would have ended up there too!

DON

Sure would like to find out more about her and what happened to her.

JACK

I've often thought about her!

MIKE

Any idea how to follow-up on this?

JACK

There was a black church down on Main Street. Still there I think. Probably the only place to start.

MIKE

Thanks Jack!

JACK

Let me know how you go will you? It's been a weighing on me ... You know!

MIKE

Sure! If we find anything! You've been a big help.

JACK

(appearing a bit more at ease)
Thanks for dropping in to see me. I needed to talk about this before...

Jack looks resignedly at Mike and Don. He even gazes at Lincoln and Percy, as if he could actually see them.

MIKE

Hang in there! Catch you later!

Don shakes Jack's hand and the pair leave the ward. Percy and Lincoln sort of hover around Jack's bed for a bit and then disappear too.

Don and Mike enter a restaurant overlooking the Chicago River.

Suzy looks a bit annoyed as she sees them come in.

SUZY
(looking directly at Mike)
So where did you guys get to then?

Mike looks a bit embarrassed and Don lets out a loud laugh.

DON
Just shopping around! Meeting started yet?

MIKE
We actually dropped in on an old timer to chat about the old days is all...

SUZY
Really?

MIKE
Yeah! It was pretty interesting as well.

BEN
We can have some lunch while we chat if you like. I ordered a platter with coffee and it should come any time.

DON
Cool!

Will is seen busy on his mobile phone with Emma hanging on each word.

WILL
(to the phone)
.... All I'm saying is to take some care with the new pump is all ... I know you're in charge ... yeah ... yeah ... OK, do your best, speak later!

Will clicks off the phone and stares at everyone.

WILL (cont'd)
He's a dick-head!

EMMA
It'll be alright, Hon, we'll be back soon enough...

WILL
How could he call himself a bloody farmer and not know about the centrifugal pumps and how they operate.

Will looks squarely at Ben.

WILL (cont'd)
So you can fix everything with a wave of a hand and a dollar bill dangling under my chin! I don't think so mate!

BEN

I'll replace him as soon as I can find someone better...

WILL

No! Better the devil …

Emma hands Will his hot coffee.

EMMA

It will sort itself out Hon.

BEN

Will, I'm sorry that man didn't work out, but we have bigger fish to fry, I'm telling you!

WILL

(sarcastically)

What! Bigger than my farm! That farm is my lifeline to sanity!

BEN

So is your music and this band, and we are going places! Hence this meeting!

Everyone goes silent and eye off both Will and Ben. The food platter arrives and breaks the tension somewhat.

Pretty soon everyone is munching away.

Don is seen to be a bit agitated and tries to catch Mike's eye. Frustrated, he gets up and whispers into Mike's ear.

DON

I reckon we should stay in Chicago and see what we can dig up.

MIKE

Just thinking the same thing myself.

DON

What'll we tell Ben and Will?

MIKE

Leave that to me, I'll handle it.

Don goes back to his place at the table somewhat relieved but still keeping a watchful eye on Mike.

BEN

(getting off the phone)

The deal is set to go ahead in LA if we all agree to it.

Silence reigns again in the room

BEN (cont'd)

They reckon about two weeks in their studio should see your part completed and we'll then take a bit of time in the mastering....

MIKE

When are you figuring on all of that?

BEN

The mastering?

MIKE

No! The recordings!

BEN

Two or three days' time. No point waiting is there?

MIKE

No can do Ben. I need at least a week right here in Chicago to recharge and chill out.

BEN

Are you serious?

MIKE

You betcha! What about you Don?

DON

A week should do it...

CHLOE

Do what? Let's just do the recording and get back home guys. I'm really tired you know!

MIKE

Sorry Chloe, but I need the time out. Fuck the recordings! I don't need them!

Will looks a bit strangely at Don and Mike and is a bit unsure on how to handle them.

WILL

I want to get home too guys. What's really going on here Mike?

MIKE

Not sure myself but Don and I are on a mission to find someone and I guess it's just that simple. We are going to do it!

WILL

Don?

DON

It may not take a week, Will. Don't ask me why but it's just something we got to do right now.

WILL

Maybe we can fly back to Oz and fix the farm for a bit and then meet you guys in LA when you've finished "looking".

Ben looks a little uncomfortable and nervous.

BEN

I'm not made of money guys. Sure you can do all of that at your own expense if you want, but I can't guarantee the LA thing beyond a few days.

Silence in the room. All eyes are on Mike.

MIKE

That's fine with me! Advance me a few thousand and whatever happens,
happens.

WILL

I think that suits me too!

*Chloe suddenly starts to feel that this whole gig is
unravelling before her eyes and she is nervous about it.*

CHLOE

(tentatively)

You guys are coming back to resume the gig and recordings aren't you?

*The room goes quiet as waiters take away some of the
plates and start clearing the table.*

DON

(reassuringly)

Of course we will! When Will gets back from fixing up his farm we'll be
cool to go down to LA, recordings or not.

CHLOE

You had me worried!

BEN

(acting the manager in control again)

I'll talk with the LA guys. They know about stuff that happens in most
bands. I think it will be cool.

MIKE

Thanks Ben.

He turns to Will & Emma.

MIKE (cont'd)

Good luck mate! I really wish I was going with you. Say hi to the town for
us won't you?

EMMA

(excited at going home for a bit)
You betchya!

*Will is seen on his mobile phone talking to his farm manager
back in Australia.*

WILL

(speaking into his phone)
We'll be back on Wednesday evening, so why don't you take a week off so
Emma and I can have a break alone.

Will listens intently and the smiles

WILL (cont'd)

Sounds good to me! Thanks mate!

Emma slips her arm around Will.

EMMA

All ok hon?

WILL

(nodding)

Can't wait to be in my own bed again!

24.   INT. HOTEL ROOM   **LATER THAT DAY**

Suzy and Mike are sharing an embrace.

SUZY

You know I'll be staying with you guys don't you?

MIKE

(smiling)

Wouldn't have it any other way babe!

The kiss again.

Don, knocks on the door and lets himself in.

DON

(genuinely sorry to have interrupted them)

Oh, sorry guys! I'll go if...

MIKE

It's cool man! Suzy is going to help us track those musos down.

DON

Great!

SUZY

Seventy years is a bloody long time ago!

DON

I know! What are we doing it for?

MIKE

Yeah! It's a bit weird isn't it?

The spirits of Percy and Lincoln appear more visible and look a bit excited.

PERCY

Finally man!

LINCOLN

We ain't found nobody yet!

PERCY

I know, but I got this good feeling about it is all.

LINCOLN

We'll see!

It is around ten in the morning as Suzy, Mike and Don are seen getting out of a taxi and paying the fare to the bemused cab driver.

CAB DRIVER
(concerned)
Are you sure you folks want to go here?

MIKE
(smiling)
It's cool! Thanks for the ride.

CAB DRIVER
It's your life!

Mike pays the cab driver. The cab speeds off and the three go inside the building.

It is somewhat run down and there is piano music coming from one of the rooms.

It is evident that there are no white people there and that the trio look a lot out of place.

An old lady, Vera, of about seventy, wanders up to them. She is wearing blue jeans and a very colourful shirt. A full head of grey hair with glasses on her eyes. Vera is about six feet tall and very stately.

VERA
(looking a bit surprised to see them)
Are you folks lost or something?

Suzy senses that it would be better if she spoke to Vera.

SUZY
(nervously)
Not really! You might be able to help us. My name is Suzy and we are all from down under!

VERA
From Australia?

DON
(smiling)
Aha!

VERA
Long way from home! My name is Vera, how can I help?

MIKE
(cautiously)
It's like this Vera. We are musicians playing at the Chicago Blues Bar...

VERA
So?

MIKE

We heard this story of two musicians who were killed there just after the war...

VERA

Which war are we talking about, honey?

MIKE

World War Two!

VERA

(a bit further surprised)
Seventy odd years ago!

MIKE

That's right. I know it's a bit of a long shot but there was some talk of a wife of one of those boys and this place was mentioned.

There is a bit of a silent pause as a few other people join Vera.

DON

Do you know anything about all of this?

Another silent moment with eyes searching the trio.

An older man, Ray, who must have been in his nineties, about five feet four and walking with a frame, speaks up.

RAY

Percy was a cousin of mine! We never knew what happened to them boys. Wasn't too much we could do at that time you see.

VERA

(sensing Ray is getting a bit distressed)
Now you sit down and rest yourself a bit, hear!

RAY

(sitting on a wooden bench)
Oh, I'm alright!

Lincoln and Percy are seen hovering around.

LINCOLN

(to Percy in a whisper)
Yeah! Packer will know my people too!

PERCY

He looks mighty old to me.

LINCOLN

Well, so would we be if we were still kicking!

The spirits share a chuckle

MIKE

(with a confused look on his face)
You wouldn't be Packer by some chance?

Don looks a bit bemused at that statement out of the blue and faces Mike.

DON

How weird is that! I had that thought too!

Ray starts to take a longer look at both Mike and Don. Suzy is also a bit confused.

SUZY

What's going on guys?

RAY

(also a bit confused)
Nobody's called me that in sixty years....

26.   INT. MELBOURNE TULLAMARINE AIRPORT

Will, Emma and Chloe are seen collecting their luggage from the carousel.
Bob, hugging his guitar, wanders in with Belinda in tow.

BOB

(annoyed somewhat)
I should have packed it better!

BELINDA

Next time I'll help you, love.

Bob and Belinda share a tender smile.

WILL

Ok so seven days and we do it again!

Everyone laughs and then ponders what that means.

CHLOE

Let's have dinner tomorrow night at my place...

EMMA

That sounds bloody great! I'll do a salad.

WILL

It's great to be home!

A couple of deep looks are passed around.
Bob and Belinda wander off in one direction while Will, Chloe and Emma wander off in the other direction.

27.   INT. MAIN STREET MISSION

RAY

(softly with a glint in his eyes)
In them days I was always carrying a piece. If you know what I mean!

VERA

We were all different then, Ray!

RAY

(looking at Mike)

How come you fellas know about me?

MIKE

Not sure exactly, but the fact is both Don and I have been getting sort of flashes from those times and your name sort of came up.

SUZY

You never told me all of that, hon!

MIKE

Didn't really know how to...

There is an uneasy silence in the room and Ray smiles over to the boys and waves his hands in the air.

RAY

You boys are having me on aren't you?

DON

I reckon not. We just broke a recording date to check this stuff out. Is any of Percy and Lincoln's family still around?

RAY

Percy's wife, Lucy, is still alive and living in the projects.

MIKE

Wow! Any chance to meet her?

RAY

Sure! Her daughter, Marie, looks after her now after her disaster of a marriage.

Ray laughs out loud.

RAY (cont'd)

She married a real loser!

---

28.   **INT. CHLOE'S PLACE**   **A FEW DAYS LATER**

Chloe lives on a farm, as do all the others in the band, and her property looks stunning with light rain falling down.

Will, Emma, Bob, Belinda and Chloe are having a jovial time with plenty of wine flowing.

There is an old jazz piece playing on the CD.

BELINDA

I spoke to dad this morning..

WILL

Oh yeah! How's it all going with him?

BELINDA

He's having fun in LA and sends his best.

EMMA
It all seems long ago and far away...

CHLOE
(laughing)
Sounds like a song to me!

EMMA
(seriously)
I'm not sure if I can take too much of that life.

Everybody sort of acknowledges the truth of the statement but silence reigns.

WILL
A couple of days home and it's like we never left it.

BOB
I know what you mean. It was great though!

BELINDA
(smiling tenderly at Bob)
You betya!

29.   **EXT/INT. CHICAGO PROJECTS**

Percy and Lincoln seem a bit nervous as the cab carrying Mike, Don and Suzy pulls up outside a rundown block of apartments.

CAB DRIVER
(concerned)
You want me to wait for you?

MIKE
We're good! Thanks mate!

CAB DRIVER
This is no place for the likes of you folks, you know!

MIKE
(paying the fare)
We'll be fine.

Mike, Don and Suzy pile out of the cab and make their way to the entrance of the building.

The wind has really picked up and Suzy cuddles into Mike.

SUZY
They weren't kidding about it being called the windy city.

Everyone laughs a bit to ease the tension.

PERCY
(amazed)
This looks a bit like a dump!

LINCOLN

It is what it is, I guess.

PERCY

(nervously)

Here goes!

LINCOLN

Know what you mean, brother!

Mike goes up the steps to the list of buzzers and after a short time of searching, presses one and waits.

Four hooded youths start to approach the three of them and, even though they can't see him, Lincoln stands in front of them.

LINCOLN (cont'd)

(firmly)

Move on boys! Don't fuck this up! It's nothing to do with you!

The older of the boys sort of stops in his tracks as if he sensed something of Lincoln and Percy.

OLDER YOUTH

(nervously to his other members)

Not them! We done enough already!

The older boy pushes one of the younger members back onto the street and they start to swagger off.

LINCOLN

Good boys!

Suddenly the buzzer flickers and a woman's voice is heard crackling away.

MARIE

(off camera)

You the friends of Ray?

MIKE

(speaking into the buzzer)

That's right!

MARIE

(off camera)

Come on up!

The door clicks and Mike quickly pushes it open and holds it for Suzy and Don to go in.

We see the three Aussies climb up four flights of steps till they make it to where a greying woman in her seventies is standing by her open apartment door.

MARIE (cont'd)

I guess you'd better come on in...

SUZY

Thanks! I'm Suzy and this is Mike and Don...

MARIE

(a bit suspiciously)

Aha!

Everyone goes inside the apartment.

30.   EXT. WILL'S FARM   **MORNING**

Will is fixing up a fence post as Emma comes out with a hot mug of tea.

EMMA

Get that into you.

WILL

Thanks hon. I reckon it was a fox that broke the fence and got into your garden... That's what I think anyway.

EMMA

(not seeming to care)

Maybe.

They both stare out at the beautiful lush acreage with the yellow canola starting to break into flower everywhere.

WILL

The band sure was a god's send alright...

EMMA

Isn't it funny how it all sort of clicked into place when we needed it?

WILL

(thoughtfully)

I know.

EMMA

(proudly)

And it was you, Will, who did it! I'm very proud of you, you know!

WILL

I sure couldn't have done it without you, or the guys.

EMMA

You were the one who believed it was possible and look where it has taken us.

Will and Emma hug and kiss

WILL

Back to L.A. in a few days.

Emma smiles tenderly at Will as they both resume their gaze over the farm.

Mike, Don and Suzy go into the apartment and all of them are struck by the musty smell and broken down furniture.

On the wall is a very old photo of Percy in his GI uniform with a very pretty Lucy by his side.

Mike stares at the photo for quite a time

Lucy, with the aid of an old walking frame, hobbles into the room.

LUCY
(proudly)
My man and me, in the day.

MIKE
You guys were some couple!

LUCY
(sadly)
Yes we were! Strange ain't it?

MIKE
(somewhat confused)
What is?

LUCY
Survived three terrible years of that Europe war without a scratch! Three weeks home, and...

Marie senses that Lucy is somewhat distressed and goes to her side.

MARIE
(to Lucy)
You sit here in the good chair now.

Lucy sits down and Marie looks Mike square in the face somewhat aggressively.

MARIE (cont'd)
(to Mike)
What's your game stirring her up like that?

MIKE
(concerned)
I know it may sound a bit weird, but your dad, Percy, and me are somewhat connected and just going with it...

MARIE
(laughing)
You con men sure think up crazy ways to operate in these days! We got nothing, see!

LUCY
(taking an interest)
Percy was a good man and a great piano player! What you talking about?

The spirits of Percy and Lincoln are seen hovering around Lucy.

PERCY
(whispering into Lucy's ears)
Hi babe. It's been a mighty long time.

Lucy suddenly sits upright as if she had heard Percy speaking.

LUCY
(looking straight through Mike)
Is that really you Perc'?

The spirit of Percy goes over to Marie and tries to touch her.

PERCY
(to Marie in a whisper)
I'm sure sorry I wasn't there for you as I should have been.

Suddenly Marie, who was showing a hard face to the world, softened and we see a tear forming in her eyes.

LUCY
(to Marie)
You're feeling Percy too aren't you dear?

Marie nods and slumps into a vacant chair in total disbelief of the experience she is having.

DON
(excitedly but restrained)
Wow!

SUZY
You said it!

DON
(to Lucy)
Does the name Lincoln mean anything to you?

At this point Lucy bursts out sobbing and is comforted by Marie.

LUCY
(softly)
I never liked him and Percy knew that. They were army buddies in France you know. A good musician but he had a way about him that spelt trouble.

Lincoln acknowledges the fact sadly and listens on.

LUCY (cont'd)
In those times he was mighty frustrated. In some ways I sort of respected that about him, not that it did us any good then or now.

DON
Do you know of any family of his?

LUCY

I only met him once and no-one ever came looking for him as far as I was concerned.

Lucy sighs deeply.

LUCY (cont'd)

It was a long time ago, dear.

Suzy goes over to Lucy and gives her a warm hug.

SUZY

It must have been tough on you raising a child alone.

LUCY

It was what it was. I ain't complaining.

SUZY

What did you mean when you said that now things hadn't improved with the racial nonsense?

Lucy looks incredulously at Suzy.

MARIE

(to Suzy)

Things haven't changed that much over the years, even with a black man in The White-house. He's done nothing for us!

SUZY

(surprised)

I thought....

MARIE

All we get is talk and nothing else!

*Suzy realizes she is in a topic she knows very little about
and so changes the subject.*

SUZY

We go to L.A. in a couple of days. Is there anything we can do for you and Lucy while we are around?

*Lucy shakes her head and Marie ponders the question a
bit more.*

MARIE

You all are musicians aren't you?

Suzy, Mike and Don all nod in unison.

MARIE (cont'd)

Well, my grandson, Marcus, he plays a mean keyboard in one of them downtown bars. Blues Train I think it's called. He needs a break!

Marie looks squarely at Mike and continues

MARIE (cont'd)

He's a good boy but the crowd he's running with I wouldn't be so sure of. If you can do something for him I'd be much obliged.

MiKE

We'll go down there tonight and I promise to see if there's anything I can help him with.

MARIE

(relieved and sort of smiling)

I never thought I'd be as surprised as I am right now. You all from Australia too! Koalas and kangaroos!

MIKE

It's been a journey for us too...

LUCY

(softly)

We never found Percy's body. You wouldn't happen to know anything about that as well would you?

Don and Mike share a look.

DON

He's buried under a building in The Loop. That's all we know. Sorry.

LUCY

(a bit teary)
The Loop?

---

32. INT. TULLAMARINE AIRPORT

Belinda is again distributing the passports and boarding documents.

Bob is cuddling his guitar, which is in a shiny new case.

Chloe, Will and Emma are a little bit sad to be on the road again and seem a bit down.

BELINDA

(to Chloe)

Here's your boarding pass. Smile why don't you!

CHLOE

(forcing a smile)

I'm not sure I really want to get on that plane, but show biz is everything isn't it?

The group share meaningful looks.

WILL

Not everything!

---

33. INT. BLUES TRAIN BAR - CHICAGO   **NIGHT**

Mike, Don and Suzy wander into a dimly lit club with a sign, Blues Train, and there's an old man at the door sitting on a stool.

Inside, the music is loud and hot.

DOORMAN
(chuckling away)
Ten bucks a piece and no trouble if you want to get in.

DON
(smiling as he hands over the thirty dollars)
Bet you've said that a few times before...

DOORMAN
Just a few. Make yourselves at home.

Other people were also trying to get in so Mike, Don and Suzy find an edge of the bar to perch onto and gaze at the band.

Lincoln and Percy are also seen hovering around.

PERCY
(pointing to the keyboard player)
That must be my great grandson, Marcus!

LINCOLN
Hell! You must be one old son of a bitch!

PERCY
I guess I would have been. Same as you!

LINCOLN
The horn player's pretty cool as well.

PERCY
Yeah!

LINCOLN
Something familiar about that horn as well...

PERCY
(looking around)
Sure different from our time!

The set announces a finishing song and Mike gets the bartender to send a drink over to the keyboard player when he's done.

The song finishes and as the band start to go backstage for their break, a serving girl hands Marcus a drink and points to Mike.

Marcus comes across to the bar to thank Mike.

MARCUS
(sweaty and pumped)
Thanks man! Could sure use it!

MIKE
Are you Marcus?

MARCUS
(suddenly getting serious)
Who are you?

MIKE
Friends of your mum and grandma.

MARCUS
(not believing him)
Yeah, right!

Suzy holds out her hand to Marcus, who takes it.

SUZY
It's a long story if you've got some time after the gig.

MARCUS
You sure talk funny. Musos?

MIKE
I play a bit of piano and Don here is pretty cool on the trumpet.

DON
We are from down under...

MARCUS
(a bit aggressively)
So how would you know my folks then?

MIKE
It really is a long story. My name is Mike and he is Don and she is Suzy.

Marcus swigs at the beer and eyes them off as weirdos.

MARCUS
(smirking)
Ok Mike, there's the keyboard, show me what you got!

MIKE
(shocked a bit)
Here and now?

MARCUS
(somewhat aggressively)
You says you can play! So play!

There is some canned music in the background amongst a lot of rowdy conversation as Mike wanders over to the piano, adjusts the seat and starts into one of his original pieces.
Marcus looks impressed and a few people clap after Mike finishes.

MARCUS (cont'd)
(surprised a bit)
Ok, you can play! What's the rest of it?

MIKE
(wiping his brow)
Those lights are pretty hot!

MARCUS
(smiling)
You get used to that…

MIKE
Can we talk after the gig?

MARCUS
I reckon so!

Mike goes back to his stool by the bar and a few people slap him on the back.

Fillip, the horn player, wanders back to the stage and leans over the piano.

FILLIP
(laughing)
He might be after your job, my man!

MARCUS
Yeah, right!

As the band resumes their final set, Lincoln becomes very excited.

LINCOLN
(to Percy)
I believe it's my old horn that young man is playing! I swear it's my old Besson 3X. I'd know that sound anywhere!

PERCY
How could you be so sure. There were plenty of Bessons around even in our day.

Lincoln stares at the horn and at Fillip

LINCOLN
It's mine alright!

Mike, Don and Suzy are enjoying a few drinks at the bar while Lincoln gets real close to Don and whispers in his ear.

LINCOLN (cont'd)
(to Don)
One last thing and we'll leave you guys be forever.

Don looks up from his drink and gazes around the room. Suzy notices.

SUZY
You Ok Don? You look like a cat jumped across your grave!

Suzy laughs and Don stays very serious.

DON

I'm getting another message from the other side again...

SUZY

(excited)

Go on, tell me!

Mike, by this time has picked up on the conversation and joins in.

DON

He wants me to talk to the horn player about his trumpet and where he got it from...

MIKE

Well, we've come this far.

DON

I guess so.

The set finishes and Marcus comes straight over to Mike.

MARCUS

We can have that talk now if you like.

MIKE

That's cool, but first I'd like it if that horn player could join us as well.

MARCUS

Fillip? What's he got to do with it?

MIKE

Apparently he's a part of why we're here.

MARCUS

(looking a little puzzled)

He's my best friend! I'll go get him if want.

MIKE

Yes please!

Marcus goes and gets Fillip, and as the room was now pretty empty it was a lot easier to converse and be heard once more.

Fillip comes over a bit aggressively and arrogant.

FILLIP

What the fuck's going down here?

MARCUS

(introducing Fillip)

This is Fillip, don't mind his mouthing off.

Everyone shakes hands and exchanges names

DON

(to Fillip)

Could you tell me where you got that Besson 3X from?

FILLIP
I didn't steal it if that's what you think!

DON
No not that.

Don pauses and takes a big breath.

DON (cont'd)
Did that use to belong to a player named Lincoln? Not sure of his last
name!

*All eyes are on Fillip as he begins to act mighty nervously
as he runs his fingers through his hair.*

FILLIP
How the fuck did you know that?

MARCUS
(also now interested)
Is that true Fil'?

FILLIP
Nobody! I mean NOBODY would know that!

MARCUS
What do you mean?

FILLIP
An uncle of my mother's sister!

Fillip slumps down onto a chair

FILLIP (cont'd)
He never made it back from the war and some of his gear has been
hanging around our place for ever.

Don looks him in the eye

DON
You may not believe this but Lincoln did make it through the war and got
back here only to be murdered by the mob. How does that grab you?

Fillip's eyes are a bit teary but he thinks it is part of a con.

FILLIP
(angrily)
Don't fuck with me, man!

MIKE
What Don said is true. We have been on a mission of discovery so to speak
from the day we arrived in this city.

SUZY
That's right guys. It all took place in a bar on Main Street in 1945, I swear!

DON

Spirits of these two dead guys keep getting us to uncover the past and you
two are the last pegs in the hole.

MARCUS

(suspiciously)
So what does that mean, exactly?

Everybody looks a bit puzzled at the question

MIKE

Well, one thing for sure is that we are off to L.A. Tomorrow night for a
week of recordings and if you two would like to come with us you might
find it interesting as well as a great opportunity to mingle with some top
industry people. What do you reckon?

MARCUS

(looking at Fillip)
It's all a bit too fast for me...

DON

(to Marcus)
We promised your mother to hand you a break and it's the best we can
offer. I'll cover the return airfares and you can bunk with us at the hotel.

Marcus gazes over at Fillip.

MARCUS

(to Fillip)
What do you think?

FILLIP

(smiling uneasily)
I'm game if you are! Brett and Pete can fill in for us here, such as it is.

MARCUS

I guess!

Handshakes all round as the scene closes.

---

34.   **INT. L.A. AIRPORT**

*A weary Belinda is seen fussing over the baggage carousel
with Bob, cradling his guitar, not far behind her.*

BELINDA

(frustrated)
I bet they've lost my bag!

BOB

It's early days, Bel'. I think we've role reversed!

*They both laugh a bit as Will and Emma come into view
grappling with their bags.*

EMMA

(calling out)

We've got ours! Have you seen Chloe?

BELINDA

(calling back)

Lucky you! Chloe went to the loo, only waiting for one lousy bag of mine.

EMMA

(smiling)

There's always one! Remember Chicago, it took an extra twenty five minutes for Will to get his!

Belinda suddenly sees her bag and squeals with joy as Chloe rocks up.

CHLOE

Must have been something I ate. Went straight through me!

EMMA

You Ok now?

CHLOE

(nodding)

I think a hot bath and decent bed will do the trick. Are we good to go?

BELINDA

(calling happily)

We are now!

The group slowly make their way to the exit and disappear from view.

---

35.   INT. RECORDING STUDIO   NEXT DAY

The building is a lavish affair with passageways leading to multiple studios.

Marcus & Fillip are seen being introduced to everyone and Ben has a quiet word to them while the others are tuning up.

BEN

I'm not quite sure why Mike has insisted on you guys being here. But try not to get in the way OK?

FILLIP

(starting to get a bit annoyed)

Hey, wait a minute...

MARCUS

(taking over the conversation)

Of course not Ben. It's going to work out fine, man!

Marcus takes Fillip to one side and has a gentle word in his ear.

MARCUS (cont'd)
(to Fillip)
Come on Fil', Mike told me this Ben was a good guy once we got to know him. Don't fuck it up!

FILLIP
(calming down a bit)
I'm good! I hate it when people boss me is all!

MARCUS
I know. This is a cool place alright!

FILLIP
I like Don, you know, and he told me he wanted me to play on one of the tracks this afternoon....

MARCUS
(surprised a bit)
Mike said the same thing to me too! I wonder what they are up to.

The band starts playing one of their tracks and are immediately in the groove.

Marcus and Fillip join a growing mix of people now watching in awe as the music fills the control room.

STUDIO TECHNICIAN
(to Will through the desk mike)
Percussion needs a bit more oomph if you get me. Sounding real cool though so I guess we'll go for a take. I'll count you in. One, two, three four!

Music starts up again and we see Will concentrating real hard while the others are a bit more lay back.

The lights on the recording console are all flashing as the technician fiddles with a few knobs.

BEN
(to the technician)
How cool is that!

STUDIO TECHNICIAN
It's old school all right...

MARCUS
(to Fillip)
That tune is mighty familiar to me but from where?

FILLIP
De ja vu. Don is playing a mean horn too!

The song finishes and the tech beckons them to come into the control room.

STUDIO TECHNICIAN
(through the mike)
Come on in here guys that was great! Take a listen through the speakers in here!

The band pile into the control room and the track starts up.

The Tech fiddles with a few knobs as it plays.

Ben has a big "told you so" look on his face.

Chloe looks a little troubled.

CHLOE
(to the Tech)
I know I can do it better! Any chance to lay another vocal track down?

STUDIO TECHNICIAN
(smiling)
Sure! I reckon you nailed it though!

CHLOE
(nervously)
Do you?

The Tech gives her the thumbs up.

STUDIO TECHNICIAN
Pop the cans on when you get back in and I'll set the volumes.

Chloe goes back into the studio alone and does her vocal line again.

She wanders back in to the control room smiling.

CHLOE
That one's better!

STUDIO TECHNICIAN
You betya! I'll get them both into the mix and with the reverb, you won't know what hit you!

Everyone laughs!

MIKE
(turning to Marcus & Fillip)
Your turn now! Get in there and see what you can do too!

MARCUS
(excited)
For real?

MIKE
Yep!

Marcus and Fillip go into the studio and don the headphones.

BEN
(to Mike)
What's going on Mike?

MIKE
You'll see!

Mike whispers to the Tech.

MIKE (cont'd)

*Two new tracks for these guys and take out my piano and
Don's trumpet from the mix you send to them, will you?*

STUDIO TECHNICIAN

(a little confused)
Sure Mike! Can't spend too much time messing around though...

MIKE

Trust me!

*After a couple of false starts, the boys get into the groove
and it is magnificent.*

STUDIO TECHNICIAN

(to Marcus & Fillip)
Come on in! That was wild!

MIKE

(to Ben)
That's some playing Ben! These guys are the real deal!

BEN

(suspiciously)
What game are you playing now, Mike?

*Marcus and Fillip come back into the control beaming from
ear to ear.*

FILLIP

That was some experience!

BEN

Damn good if you ask me!

MARCUS

(to Mike)
Thanks Mike. I'm not sure why you dragged us here, but this is a career
highlight for me, that's for sure!

MIKE

(quietly to Marcus)
The best is yet to come.

*The track starts to play back and everyone is amazed at
what the Tech is doing as he mixes both piano parts as well
as both trumpet parts in and out.*

STUDIO TECHNICIAN

(excitedly)
There's a unique sound happening here. I reckon it might take me a few
extra days to get it right, but it will be worth it!

*Everyone is a little awe struck by what they are listening
to and Mike gives some sheet music to Marcus from his
briefcase.*

MIKE

(to Marcus and Fillip)
Take a look at this. It's the next piece we're doing.

Ben notices the exchange and says nothing to them.

STUDIO TECHNICIAN
Will, are you guys ready for the next recording?

A lot of mumbles as Will leads the band back into the studio and they get themselves ready.

Suddenly the control booth is filled with music and singing as Marcus and Fillip study the music, note by note.

FILLIP

(to Marcus quietly)
That's a harmony line...

MARCUS

(quietly)
I know.

Suzy goes over to the two boys.

SUZY

You guys are great! Did you know how good you were?

MARCUS

My head's spinning! What's with Mike doing all this for us?

SUZY

Not sure! You just go with it is all I can suggest!

FILLIP

(chiming in)
Too easy!

Montage of shots as Marcus and Fillip go in to the studio, after the band finishes each song, to lay down their tracks and revel in the atmosphere.

36.	INT. HOTEL ROOM	LATER THAT EVENING

Mike and Suzy are having a quiet time lying on the bed, in a gentle embrace.

MIKE

(seriously)
Suzy, I'm planning to leave the band after the recordings are done...

SUZY

(surprised)
What!

MIKE

Yep! It's been a heap of fun but the truth is I really miss home and the farm, and...

SUZY

(interrupting him)

I thought something was going on in that mind of yours when you bought
Marcus and Fillip to L.A.

Mike looks tenderly at her.

MIKE

(smiling)

You know me pretty well.

SUZY

(calculating)

Four of five days' time! Have you told Will or Don as yet?

MIKE

Don and I feel the same way and figured not to rock the boat until the
recordings were done.

SUZY

Mmm!

MIKE

(serious again)

How would you like to be a farmer's wife?

*Suzy stares at Mike for a long time and there are tears in
her eyes.*

SUZY

Only if that farmer is you!

MIKE

(excited and relieved)

Do you mean it?

SUZY

(happily)

Of course I do! I just can't picture myself with anyone else!

They embrace and kiss madly

MIKE

What about Ben?

SUZY

Don't worry, dad will understand. I'll handle it!

37.   INT. RECORDING STUDIO

*It's the last day of recordings and Marcus and Fillip are
putting the finishing touches to the final song.*

*Don takes Mike outside the control room into the passage
way and has a private chat with him.*

DON

Are we still going through with it?

MIKE

You betya!

DON

How are we going to break it to Will?

MIKE

Leave it to me, mate. By the way, Suzy and I are going to get hitched and
I'd sure feel good if you'd be the best man!

Don bursts out laughing as he slaps Mike affectionately.

DON

Wow! You old dog!

MIKE

It's love! What else can I do?

DON

(happily)
I'd be honoured, mate!

*Don and Mike wander back into the control room as
Marcus and Fillip arrive as well.*

STUDIO TECHNICIAN

(seriously)
This is going to be some album!

BEN

(relieved)
I'm surprised we got it done in the time.

STUDIO TECHNICIAN

If you want me to master the tracks I'll start in about two weeks' time.

BEN

Why the wait?

STUDIO TECHNICIAN

My ears! I'm so full on with the songs that anything I touch won't be worth
a pinch of shit! Excuse my French! I need the time to clear my brain and do
it properly.

BEN

I see!

STUDIO TECHNICIAN

Don't sweat it Ben, it's the way it should be done if you want a top job, and
believe me, these tracks deserve it!

BEN

(a bit disappointed)
Ok! I guess you know what you're doing better than me!

STUDIO TECHNICIAN

On this, yes! Don't worry, it's going to be great!

Don wanders up to Ben and the Tech

DON

Great sessions! Celebration tonight in my suite at seven and I'd like you both to be there!

STUDIO TECHNICIAN

Sorry Don, no can do! Working tonight!

BEN

I'll be there!

DON

Cool! See you then!

Don walks out of the control room with Mike and the others and disappears from view.

---

38.   **INT. DON'S ROOM**   **LATER THAT NIGHT**

Everyone is crammed into Don's hotel room with plenty of drinks and chips.

Ben comes and joins the party.

BEN

Sorry I'm late guys! You know what it's like!

DON
(smiling)
Better late than never!

Ben gets handed a drink and he starts into it almost immediately.

MIKE
(tapping his beer bottle)
You're probably wondering why I called this meeting!

CHLOE
(laughing and calling out)
You didn't!

Everyone cracks up laughing.

MIKE
(seriously)
Actually, I did!

Don turns the CD player off and all eyes are on Mike as Suzy moves up and takes his hand.

MIKE (cont'd)
(looking at Will)
There's two things I want to say. Before I do though, how good has the past week been!

Will shuffles around nervously

WILL
It's all been magic! What's going on Mike?

MIKE
Don and I are leaving the band and going home...

CHLOE
(surprised)
You are kidding! Aren't you?

MIKE
(shaking his head)
Not this time Chloe.

WILL
(a little shaken)
What's the second thing?

MIKE
(looking at Ben)
Suzy and I are going to tie the knot.

Mike and Suzy kiss.

Ben looks a bit stunned.

BEN
(slowly)
About time too, if you ask me!

Suzy goes up to Ben and throws her arms around him as Belinda joins them.

SUZY
(a bit teary)
What do you think, dad?

Ben is sort of lost for words for a minute.

BELINDA
(hugging Suzy)
Good for you Suzy! When are you planning it for?

SUZY
Next month, back home on Mike's, our, farm. You are all invited! Don is going to be the best man!

A lot of hugs and kisses and handshakes from everyone.
Will looks over to Ben and they share a couple of meaningful looks.

WILL
(to Don)
So that's why you had Marcus and Fillip come down here.

DON
It's perfect Will! Fillip's a heap better player than me ...

WILL

We've been friends all our lives...

DON

And we'll always be friends, mate! Nothing will ever change that!

WILL

(thoughtfully)

You probably **did** what I've been considering but couldn't afford to...

DON

We wouldn't have got this far without you, Will!

*Will acknowledges and lets the changing situation sink
into his psyche a bit.*

BEN

(mumbling to himself)

It's all starting to make some sense now!

Marcus and Fillip look at each other nervously.

FILLIP

(to Marcus)

What's your take on all of this?

MARCUS

Seems too good to be true! This band and those recordings are a couple of
levels up from where we were.

FILLIP

A week ago...

MARCUS

I know!

Ben starts to feel a bit nervous and goes over to Mike.

BEN

I guess it's welcome to the family time!

MiKE

(hugging Ben)

Thanks dad!

Belinda joins in as they all have a little chuckle.

BELINDA

(laughing)

Hey Bro'!

Suzy goes over to Marcus.

MARCUS

(to Suzy)

Congrats!

SUZY

Thanks Marcus. Mike and I would love to have you both come to our wedding in Oz you know!

MARCUS

It's a long way...

FILLIP

We better get passports then I guess.

SUZY

Belinda will handle it all if you'd like.

FILLIP

Cool!

SUZY

I bet Lucy's never been on a plane in her life!

MARCUS

Probably not...

SUZY

I'd sure like Lucy and Marie to be our guests as well if you could ask them for me.

MARCUS

I'll ask, but don't hold your breath. They don't go no-where!

Belinda comes to them and gives Suzy a big hug and smooches a kiss.

BELINDA

(bubbly)
So you're going to beat me to the altar after all?

SUZY

(laughing)
Looks that way! How are you and Bob traveling?

BELINDA

(somewhat serious)
Not sure! He's such a complex insect.

SUZY

How so?

BELINDA

I know he loves me and all, but he has a problem in actually saying the words.

SUZY

Mike is totally different to that! Sometimes I reckon he just goes through a routine of phrases he thinks I'll love. And I do!

BELINDA

But he does love you! You can just tell!

SUZY

(tenderly)

Yep! He's a sweety alright!

*Ben wanders over to his daughters with a concerned look
on his face.*

BEN

Great news Suzy!

SUZY

What's up dad?

BEN

We have three weeks solid bookings here in LA and then the album promo
and release! It's all happening at the same time!

BELINDA

(smiling)

Just the way you like it! No-one revels in pressure situations like you, Ben!

Ben sort of smiles.

BEN

(to Suzy)

When and where are you planning the wedding?

SUZY

Four weeks from today on Mike's farm! You **will** be walking me down the
aisle, won't you?

BEN

(smiling)

Of course I will!

BELINDA

(to Ben)

Why don't you arrange some gigs in Melbourne and make it a business
trip?

They all laugh. Ben thinks about it for a bit.

BEN

(to himself)

Not a bad idea at that!

---

39.   INT. L.A. AIRPORT

*Mike, Suzy and Don are seen walking through the customs
area and onto the plane.*

The plane takes off.

---

40.   INT. THE LATIN QUARTER IN LA

*Will and the boys are belting out one of the album tracks
to an enthusiastic crowd.*

Belinda is sitting at the bar with Ben who is seen talking into his mobile phone.

Ben finishes his call just as the set finishes.

BELINDA

(excitedly)

How great are these guys!

BEN

(smiling)

I knew it the first time I saw them in that pub!

BELINDA

Yeah, but they've improved heaps from that!

BEN

I know!

Ben takes a sip on his beer.

BEN (cont'd)

Just signed them for two weeks in Paris!

BELINDA

When for?

BEN

Don't worry! Straight after the wedding!

BELINDA

(somewhat relieved)

How bloody brilliant is that! And those two boys just click with the band, don't you think?

BEN

Yep! Pretty amazing all round, if you ask me!

---

41.   INT. HOTEL DINING ROOM BACK IN AUSTRALIA   EVENING

Mike and Don wander into the local hotel and sit at the bar waiting for John to come and serve them.

JOHN

(not really recognizing them)

What can I get you two?

DON

(casually)

Hi John.

JOHN

(slowly)

G'day!

Suddenly he realizes who it is.

JOHN (cont'd)

Shit! Don! Mike! How the hell are you!

MIKE

(smiling)

G'day mate!

JOHN

Beer?

DON

Get one for yourself while you order us a couple of your rib eye steaks!

JOHN

Sure!

MiKE

(calling out to John)

Medium rare!

Don and Mike go over to a table and John joins them carrying the beers on a tray.

JOHN

Big time now! I saw Will about three weeks back too! How long are you going to be in town?

MIKE

(laughing)

About fifty years I'd say!

JOHN

(puzzled)

Yeah!

MIKE

Well, actually Don and I have quit the band and I'm getting married in a couple of weeks' time!

JOHN

(astonished)

You don't say!

DON

Yep! I'm the best man!

JOHN

(toasting Mike)

Here's to you! So where's the lucky lady?

MiKE

Suzy's in Melbourne seeing friends and organizing stuff, you know.

John swigs on his beer letting it all sink in.

JOHN

So where is the wedding going to be?

MIKE

Right here mate! It's where we met and I guess we'll need ten rooms for
the night of the twenty third!

JOHN

You got it Mike!

They all clink glasses and down the beers.

42.   **INT. MIKE'S HOUSE**   **NEXT DAY**

*The rain is lightly falling on the fields of wheat that are
gently blowing in the wind.*

*Suzy is at the stove making a coffee and brings a mug over
to where Mike is lounging around.*

Mike takes the mug and smiles at Suzy.

MIKE

Thanks babe!

*Mike sips tentatively at the steaming coffee somewhat
deep in thought.*

MIKE (cont'd)

(tenderly)

Can you believe we are going to be married in a couple of days?

SUZY

(kissing him)

It's too mad to even think about it!

MIKE

(somewhat seriously)

I know! It could all be a dream and I am going to wake up, alone and
without you!

SUZY

(pinching him)

It's no dream!

*The phone starts ringing and they both just watch it ring
and ring till it stops.*

MIKE

I would NEVER have done that a year ago!

SUZY

(laughing)

I do it all the time!

*The phone starts ringing again and this time Mike grabs it
before it stops.*

149

MIKE
(into the phone)
Mike here!

We hear Will on the other end of the line.

WILL
(off screen)
Hi Mike! We're back and I have a copy of the CD for you as well!

MIKE
(to Suzy, holding his hand over the mouthpiece)
It's Will! He's back!

Mike releases his grip on the phone piece, and speaks into it.

MiKE (cont'd)
Great to hear your voice Will! How you doing? How's the band?

WILL
(off screen)
Tired, but all good! Going to crash now but how about we drop by tomorrow arvo for a coffee?

MIKE
Sounds like a plan! Catch you then!

Mike hangs up the phone and the scene fades out.
The scene is now the next afternoon as Will and Emma are seen knocking on Mike's front door and then letting themselves in.

EMMA
(calling out)
You guys decent?

Suzy wanders in smiling, dressed in denim working jeans with a band T-shirt on.

SUZY
(hugging them both)
Mike's coming! He's been fixing a pump and is now getting cleaned up.

WILL
There's always a job around the corner on a farm!

SUZY
I'll get used to that!

EMMA
So tomorrow's the big day! How exciting!

SUZY
(laughing)
I actually can't wait for it to be all over. If you know what I mean?

EMMA

Sure do!

Mike wanders in and hugs both Will and Emma.

MiKE

(sincerely)

So good to see you guys!

WILL

We missed you mate! You, Don and Suzy not being there was kinda weird!

*Will hands the CD over to Mike who straight away puts in
on his player.*

The music sounds great!

MIKE

Wow! We were pretty good!

A lot of nods all round.

43.   INT. TOWN CHURCH

*Inside the church we see Bob and Belinda sitting with
Marcus, Fillip, Marie and Lucy.*

Chloe and her fella is a couple of rows back.

*The little church is packed and there is a lot of cheering and
clapping as the priest continues.*

PRIEST

(looking at Mike and Suzy)

I now pronounce you man and wife! Mike, you may now kiss the bride!

Mike does just that and the cheering erupts again.

44.   EXT. TOWN'S MAIN STREET

*Mike and Suzy lead the procession as they march the
hundred or so meters to the hotel.*

*At the entrance to the hotel is a big banner "Where there's
a Will" tonight @ 8! All welcome!*

45.   INT. HOTEL DINING ROOM

*Tables and chairs are all decked out in white and blue with
wildflowers and orchids on every table.*

*Everyone is sitting down eating and drinking as Don reads
out a few telegrams and tells some dirty stories of Mike
and his past.*

DON

(laughing mid-speech)

.... we were so wasted by then, both of us ended up sleeping in the barn
with the prize cow!

Everyone laughs.

DON (cont'd)
I know I was sick for days after that! Mike just took it in his stride! I never knew how he did it!

Everyone laughs again!

DON (cont'd)
(raising his glass)
To Mike and Suzy!

A lot of clapping as Suzy takes Mike onto the dance floor and encourages everyone to join in too.

SUZY
(calling out)
Come on!

Pretty soon quite a lot of people are bopping along to the recorded music in the background.
Marcus is dancing with Marie and Fillip very gently is sort of standing on the dance floor with Lucy, who looks radiant.
Ernie and a few of the townspeople start flocking into the hotel.
Ben goes over to speak with Ernie.

BEN
(genuinely)
Wife not here tonight, Ernie?

ERNIE
(smiling)
Never got around to marriage and all of that.

BEN
(laughing)
Well you had me fooled!

ERNIE
(laughing)
So how is the old Merc'?

BEN
Not a day's trouble since! That job you did on her and me, worth every penny mate!

Ben and Ernie share a laugh together and watch as the song finishes and the dancers go back to their seats.
John goes up to the stage and taps the microphone a few times.

JOHN
The last time we had Will and the boys all together I told him it would be their last gig here..

Whistles and cheering.

JOHN (cont'd)
Well that night was a game changer alright!

More whistles.

JOHN (cont'd)
(speaking directly to Will)
How about it Will? For old times' sake.

Will acknowledges the request and winks at the rest of the band, who are already making their way onto the stage.
Will notices that Marcus and Fillip haven't moved in their seats.

WILL
(to Marcus and Fillip)
Come on guys, you're a part of this band now!

MARCUS
(calling back)
We're on strike, mate! You better get Mike and Don for this one!

Mike and Don, to the cheers of the locals, get up and join the band for a final session.
The band starts up with one great song after another.
Closing credits start to roll onto the screen.

BEN
(whispering to Suzy and Belinda)
First time I heard them I knew they would be great!

SUZY AND BELINDA
(laughing)
Sure Dad!

THE END

THE THIRD PLAYER

1.	INT FOOTBALL STADIUM	AFTERNOON

Bill Watson, well dressed, late twenties, watches disappointedly as his team is getting thrashed. He gazes occasionally at his footy record, marking the next opposition goal in the column and continues to watch the game in virtual silence compared to the rowdy spectators all around him.

2.	INT. FOOTBALL CLUB ROOMS	

Proud faces stare out from old photographs that line the walls.

3.	EXT. BUS STOP	MINUTES LATER

Bill waits at a bus stop.

4.	INT. OFFICE SETTING	SAME TIME

A well-dressed man is alone in his office on the phone.

WELL-DRESSED MAN
I don't smell the fire ... what's the hold-up?

JIMMY RIVERS
(off screen on the phone)
OK! OK! I'm on to it.

WELL-DRESSED MAN
Well, when exactly did you have in mind?

JIMMY RIVERS
She'll be sweet. Don't worry!

WELL-DRESSED MAN
My money's in your pocket son, or have you forgotten that...

JIMMY RIVERS
Nah! Two weeks she'll be sweet.

WELL-DRESSED MAN
I'm not someone you can fuck around with!

5.	INT/EXT BUS	SAME TIME

Bill gets on a bus and takes a seat at the back. He looks blankly out at the suburban vista.

A big street in a busy suburb of a country town. Bill gets off the bus and just ambles along the pathway, somewhat deep in thought. A very old Aboriginal lady is seen standing at a zebra crossing waiting for the walk signal. She starts to stumble and collapse and is caught in flight by Bill.

BILL

(Concerned)
You OK?

POSS

(Spluttering)
I can't breathe.

BILL

Just sit down here for a bit

Bill quickly dials his mobile phone.
Emergency? I've got an old lady collapsed here, could be her heart .... OK ... corner of Drummond and Station .... Thanks.

Bill (cont'd to Poss)

They'll be here in a tick.

A few people stop and stare. An ambulance arrives. Poss gets put in. Bill climbs in with her.

7.   **INT/EXT AMBULANCE**

With the sirens wailing, and Bill sitting next to Poss, the ambulance speeds off into the distance.

8.   **INT HOSPITAL FRONT DESK**   **3PM**

Bill stands at the front desk of a local hospital, as Poss get wheeled past on a trolley. Nurses and admin staff hover around asking questions. There is a lot of background inaudible sound. Bill has a vacant look on his face and after shrugging his shoulders, walks out of the main doors into the open air.

9.   **INT. FOOTBALL CLUB ROOMS**

The proud faces in the old photographs appear to be showing some emotion.

10.   **INT STADIUM**   **EVENING**

Big city stadium, very flashy (up market) flood lit with a footy team training hard. Two officials are chatting in the stands while watching the training.

OFFICIAL ONE

(yelling out)

Good one Thommo!

OFFICIAL TWO

Bloody champions at training aren't they. Why can't the buggers do it in a
game, for goodness sakes?

OFFICIAL ONE

Beats me!

(yelling out again)

It's called a handball, son! Kick the flaming thing!

OFFICIAL TWO

I don't think they even know what to do when they get the bloody ball.

OFFICIAL ONE

Thank God there's only 2 weeks to go! I suppose we'll have to sack the
coach again?

OFFICIAL TWO

Yeah, same old story! But on the bottom for the third year in a row!

OFFICIAL ONE

Do you think I hadn't noticed?

OFFICIAL TWO

What do you reckon we can do about it?

OFFICIAL ONE

I've thought about it, but we just haven't got the talent!

OFFICIAL TWO

I know! But if we could buy some Melbourne ex's you know.

OFFICIAL ONE

Dream on, dream on!

(yelling out to the team)

Go and get the ball son! Crikey Moses, where do they find these so called
players?

OFFICIAL TWO

(Sarcastically)

You hired 'em!

(laughs)

We just got to put up with 'em!

---

11. EXT OLD FOOTY GROUND   **EVENING**

*An old run down footy ground. The camera goes into the
changing rooms and deserted board rooms. About 10
large photographs are still on the walls there and a close-
up shows them to be the first 10 premiership sides dating
back 100 years or more. The faces of the past heroes look
proudly and somewhat troubled across a vacant room.*

*Bill wanders into the hospital ward and takes a seat near
Poss's bed, and waits till she opens her eyes.*

BILL

(cheerily)
G'day mate … feeling better?

POSS

(Rubbing her eyes)
Who are you? Oh yeah! Thanks mate!

BILL

You had us worried there a bit.

POSS

Yeah! I'm alright.

BILL

Yeah! I can see that!
(laughs a bit)

POSS

How long have I been here? Do you know?

BILL

Couple of days! I brought you in on Saturday.

POSS

(sighing)
Don't tell me!
(She takes a deep breath and)
Oh lord! It's Tuesday, isn't it?

Poss starts getting very agitated, and Bill tries to pacify her.

BILL

(In a consoling manner)
Yeah, so? Where you got to go?

POSS

(Cursing under her breath)
Bloody hell!

BILL

(Genuinely interested)
What's the matter? Is there anything I can do, or call someone?

POSS

(Quite sadly and resignedly)
No! They don't care anymore.

BILL

(concerned)
Your family?

POSS

(Ignoring the question and looking straight at Bill in a pleading fashion.)
Can you do me a favour son?

BILL

If I can. What is it?

POSS

There's a bunch of keys attached to my belt over there. Go get them will you?
(Bill gets them from the cupboard and hands them to Poss.)
These are for the footy ground. Every Tuesday and Thursday the doors must be unlocked for training at four. Please!

BILL

What ground is that then?

POSS

It's the one on William's Road, you can't miss it.

BILL

Is that the old ground for the club?

POSS

(Getting somewhat distressed)
Please promise me son! To keep the training days schedule. Please! I promised them!

A nurse comes into the room, and Bill is staring directly at Poss, noticing how upset she had become all of a sudden.

BILL

(looking at his watch)
OK. Oh, it's quarter past four now. I better go then! I'll see you later.

POSS

(Somewhat relieved)
You won't forget will you?

BILL

(Heading quickly to the door)
Nah, she'll be right. I'm on my way.

---

13. EXT CARPARKING AREA

Bill rushes out and gets into his car.

14. INT BILL'S CAR

We see him driving to the ground.

15. EXT THE OLD GROUND   4.30 PM

Bill fossicks and tries a few keys at the gate. One works, and then he does the same on the main door.

16. INT THE CLUB ROOMS

Bill goes inside, plays with light switches and to his amazement, all the lights work, even on the ground.

17. INT THE CLUB ROOM   6.35 PM

There is a big clock in the main entrance, and after two hours of exploration and waiting, Bill locks up the place and leaves.

18. INT THE CLUB ROOM   SOME TIME LATER

The camera goes back to the old photos on the wall and slowly the scene goes to sepia as the players (spirits of the past) break free from their prisons and come to life, stepping out of their frames in the football gear of a bygone age. They start talking to each other about the demise of their club. Notable is the spirit that emerges from a dusty picture titled Eric Morgan, the captain coach of the 1895 and 1896 premiership teams.

SPIRIT 1

What's happening?

ERIC

We are in a moment of time.

SPIRIT 2

Is it real?

ERIC

Only for us, and only in this moment.

SPIRIT 3

Eric, what's really going on?

ERIC

(a wry smile on his face)

Fellas, our club's in trouble. We can help to teach the current players the basics of what it takes to being an Aussie Rules footballer.

All the spirits look a bit bewildered, but no-one says a word to interrupt the coach.

ERIC (cont'd)

I love this club!

All the spirits gather around Eric with somewhat worried looks on their faces

ERIC (cont'd)

I've arranged a pardon, of sorts, for three of us for one year.

The spirit players mumble and lot of discussion ensues.

ERIC (cont'd)

Whoever we decide and choose, will be able to enter the body and soul of a living human for exactly one year. Why don't we think on it tonight and tomorrow choose them? Oh yeah, these living humans have to actually come here to be entered. That's the deal.

19. INT. THE CLUB ROOM   **JUST BEFORE SUNRISE**

The past players mumble to themselves and the camera fades. The sunlight outside starts streaming through the window as it gradually becomes morning.

ERIC (cont'd)

Well how did you all do?

SPIRIT 1

From my team in 1938, Garry Johnson only played 45 games before the war killed him, he was the best full forward I have ever seen.

The spirits grunt their approval.

SPIRIT 2

Bloody war took some good boys alright.

ERIC

I remember him, I always thought he never had much of a chance, good choice.

(looking directly over to Garry)

Garry, are you ready for this, you know what's at stake.

GARRY

I am Eric. Thanks guys I won't let you down.

SPIRIT 2

I'm from the '76 team, and Snowy Reynolds is our pick for a rover. Fastest kid on the block. What do ya reckon?

SPIRIT 3

He'd sure show these guys a thing or two over ten yards.

ERIC

(a bit more concerned in his speech)

Yes, I can see where you're all coming from. But there's more to footy than sheer speed, Snowy. You were real good on the field, and no-one will deny that, but there were times my boy when you let it get to you. You know what I mean? You can't let that happen this time! Can you do what's asked of you today, and it's a big ask?

SNOWY

(Very soberly in speech)

I can Eric, yeah. I've got something to prove. To myself. Thanks guys for having the faith in me. I'll do my bit, yeah, you can count on that!

ERIC

So far so good! I approve! Who's next?

SPIRIT 3

Eric, you've got to be the third player!

Everyone acknowledges and even Eric is a bit humbled by the response.

SPIRIT 3 (cont'd)

You were the best of us.

At this everyone starts clapping the three nominated spirits and singing the club theme song as the scene fades out.

20. INT DELICATESSEN OPPOSITE THE OLD GROUND   6:15PM

A young 19 year old Aboriginal boy, Ken Merryman, is sweeping the floor. Bill comes in and goes up to the counter where an older lady serves him.

BILL

Cup of white coffee thanks luv.

Bill is handed his coffee and as he is drinking, the boy comes over and says hello.

KEN

Hey! You don't remember me do ya?

BILL

Wait a minute!

KEN

I was in your class three years back, yeah.

BILL

Ken Merryman!

KEN

(beaming)
That's me, yeah! What ya doing 'round here?

BILL

(pointing to the ground across the road)
Looking after it for a bit.

KEN

Oh yeah!

BILL

So you working here now are you?

KEN

Yeah!

Bill finishes his drink and is about to leave when he gets a thought and comes back to Ken.

BILL

Say, could you keep an eye on the ground for me while I'm at school, and if
you see any trouble, call me?

KEN

Yeah, I can do that.

Bill gives him a card with his number on it and turns to go.

BILL

(yelling over shoulder)
Thanks, see you!

KEN

(to the lady behind the counter)
That fella used to be my teacher a couple of years back.

COUNTER LADY

(sarcastically)
Didn't teach you much then did he?

21. EXT THE DELI	**SATURDAY NIGHT**

*Ken is locking the door getting ready to go on home. Looking
across the road he notices a shadow of a person jump the
gate of the old ground, push the main door open and go in.*

22. INT THE DELI

*Quickly Ken goes back inside the delicatessen and finds
Bill's card and rings him.*

23. EXT THE DELI

Soon after, Bill arrives and goes over to Ken.

BILL

Has he come out yet?

KEN

Nope! Still there, yeah, unless he's out the other side.

BILL

I better take a look.

KEN

(Smiling)
I'll come with ya yeah. Ya might need a hand, eh?

*They both grin at each other and gingerly go across the
road.*

24. EXT THE OLD GROUND.

*Bill and Ken carefully open the gate and then the door,
they go inside.*

Bill and Ken start turning all the lights on. They both stay together looking into each room.

KEN

Geez! I always wondered what this old joint looked like inside.

Bill sees Ken getting a little nervous.

KEN (cont'd)

Yeah! It smells alright I sort of prefer the older places, yeah!

When they get to the board room, they notice a young man (longish hair and scruffy, around mid-twenties, quite tall and lean) trying to hide behind some empty cartons.

BILL

You there! Get out here!

The man stands up and faces them in a tough stance.

BILL (cont'd)

Well? What the hell do you think you're doing here?

JIMMY RIVERS

I didn't mean to disturb anything mister! I'm no thief!

BILL

Yeah! Well what's your story then?

JIMMY RIVERS

What do you care....

BILL

Well!

JIMMY RIVERS

I live here, see....

BILL

Do you think I came down in the last shower?

JIMMY RIVERS

It's true! Bloody hell! I didn't think anyone would mind.
(looking straight at Bill)
I've seen you here before. Bloody hell!

BILL

Out of work too, I suppose?

JIMMY RIVERS

What do you think?

The three spirits of Eric, Garry and Snowy materialise in the room.

ERIC

What do you think, boys?

SNOWY
Are you serious?

GARRY
A whole year in them....

ERIC
Fussy buggers!

SNOWY
Yeah, just look at them!

ERIC
Oh they'll be alright. What about it Garry?

GARRY
The things I do for this club, I don't know!

ERIC
Good boys! It'll be fine!

BILL
(softened by the plea)
Look mate, you can't stay here.

JIMMY RIVERS
Ok! I'll go...

BILL
I've got a room at the back of my place you can use.

Suddenly the lights flicker and the scene turns to sepia as the three spirits enter Bill, Ken and Jimmy. They involuntarily freeze for a moment, then come to, looking startled.

BILL (cont'd)
What the hell was that?

KEN
It's a bit weird in here aint it?

BILL
Know what you mean.

JIMMY RIVERS
Are you serious about that room?

Bill nods and the three men leave the ground.

---

26. INT BILL'S BEDROOM   **NIGHT**

Bill is having a very restless night with vivid images of tense football matches.

27. INT KEN'S BEDROOM   **SAME NIGHT**

Ken experiencing similar things to Bill.

<table><tr><td>**28. INT JIMMY'S BEDROOM**</td><td>**SAME NIGHT**</td></tr></table>

Jimmy experiencing similar things to the other two.

<table><tr><td>**29. INT HOSPITAL - RECEPTION DESK**</td><td>**MORNING**</td></tr></table>

RECEPTIONIST

Excuse me, are you the one who brought Mrs Robinson in last week?

BILL

If you mean the old lady last Saturday, I am! Is she Ok?

RECEPTIONIST

Just wait a minute please, doctor wants a word with you.

BILL

Ok.

RECEPTIONSIST

Doctor! This is the man who brought Mrs Robinson in.

DOCTOR

Thanks Tess. How do you do?

BILL

Not bad thanks. How's she doing?

DOCTOR

I'm afraid she's had a bit of a stroke and will have to stay here for a bit until she's better than she is now.

BILL

Sorry to hear that.

DOCTOR

Yes, well we don't really know much about her, and I was hoping you might fill in the gaps.

BILL

No I'm afraid not. I sort of caught her in the street, so to speak, and you probably know more than me now. You could try the football club, they might help.

DOCTOR

Well if you do find her family or friends, please let me know, and don't stay too long this visit, she needs her rest.

BILL

I'll do what I can.

30. INT HOSPITAL - POSS'S ROOM

Bill walks into the room expecting the worst, to see Poss sitting up reading the newspaper. Floating in with him is the spirit of Snowy Robinson.

BILL

I'm not disturbing you am I?

POSS

Oh it's you! Sit down over here, yeah.

BILL

I can't stay long, but the ground's OK.

POSS

You keeping it open?

BILL

Yeah, yeah! No takers yet.

POSS

Thanks son, yeah, it's important to me see. By the way what is your name?

BILL

Eric Morr… No, my name is Bill Watson. Pretty bad when a fella can't remember his own name Ha! What's yours?

POSS

Poss! Just call me Poss, everyone does now.

BILL

You gave everyone a bit of a scare the other day.

POSS

I know, yeah.

BILL

The doctors here want to know about your family and friends and things like that, do you want me to let them know you're in here, and all that?

POSS

There's no-one left of my people, I'm the last. I never thought I'd live this long anyway.

BILL

What do you mean?

POSS

Oh nothing.

The spirit of Snowy drifts out of the room, we notice tears in his eyes.

BILL

I'd like to do some training on the ground if that's OK?

POSS

Yeah, that'll be fine. You'll find some old boots and some training balls in the third cupboard down from the main store-room, yeah, along with some jumpers and other stuff. You'll find them in good nick, and if you could give 'em a clean for me after you use 'em I'd appreciate it.

BILL

Thanks Poss. You must really love that club?

POSS

Just a little, yeah. My man played there in the old days.

Poss starts to look tired. Her head droops and a NURSE enters the room. She gives Bill one of those "You'd better go" looks.

NURSE

I think we better take your BP again Mrs Robinson, eh? Your friend can see you later!

BILL

I'll catch you later Poss.

31. INT BILL'S HOME **12 NOON**

Jimmy is filling his bag with some of Bill's silverware and then rummaging through drawers taking the odd piece of jewellery. The spirit of Garry Johnson watching him with a disgusted look on his face.

Bill comes home and Jimmy quickly drops his bag off in his room and goes out to the kitchen to greet Bill.

The spirits of Garry and Eric look at each other.

GARRY

This fella is some piece of work!

ERIC

Get into his head! Yeah, speak to him with your words.

GARRY

I'll try!

ERIC

That's all I'm asking.

JIMMY RIVERS

G'day mate! I thought ya'd skipped town!

BILL

G'day! I'd almost forgotten about you! Sorry about that!

JIMMY RIVERS

I'm sweet!

BILL

I was visiting a friend in hospital ... feel like some lunch?

JIMMY RIVERS

Sounds good to me!

Bill gets some bowls out of the fridge and gently slides two plates onto the table. They are make sandwiches out of a

168

BILL

So what happened to you?

JIMMY

Lost me job! I was a storeman for the local Ford plant that closed down.
And then me mum got sick and died. I can't seem to get it together these
days.

BILL

So what have you been doing?

JIMMY

There's been no work around here for ages ....

BILL

I know!

JIMMY

Getting fit, by doing laps of that oval of yours, late at night when no-one's
around, it's sort of good fun.

BILL

Not my oval!

JIMMY

Yeah, well it's a great place to train and think, it's sort of peaceful like at
night, sort of ....

BILL

Therapy you mean?

JIMMY

Suppose so, why don't ya come with me?

BILL

What, sleep down there?
(Laughs)

JIMMY

No! Have a kick and a run.

BILL

Funny you mentioning it because the old lady who looks after the place
said we could use some of the gear, and I wouldn't mind to stretch my legs
a bit. You up for it this afternoon some time?

JIMMY

That'll be sweet! What sort of work do ya do then?

BILL

I'm a science teacher at the local high school. Been there for four years
now.

JIMMY

So ya permanent are ya?

BILL

I sure hope they think so.

JIMMY

Ya like it, do ya?

BILL

(serious all of a sudden)
Yes I do! When you can make a difference to someone's life for the better.
Makes all the other stuff worthwhile. If you get my drift.

*They both nod at each other and go back to hoeing their
food down in a hungry fashion.*

JIMMY

Yeah, I remember me old maths teacher, he was alright too.

32. EXT OLD FOOTY GROUND   EARLY AFTERNOON

*We cut to the footy ground. It's around 2:30 on a sunny
day where Bill and Jimmy are out kicking a football and
doing some routines. The ball is noticeably being kicked a
long distance and Bill goes into the goal square beckoning
Jimmy to have a few shots at goal. From beyond the 50
yard line and on all angles, Bill is a little in awe as goal
after goal is kicked. He calls out a few times "great shot"
and "fair go"!*

33. INT THE CLUB ROOM   SOME TIME LATER

*After the session they clean the balls and boots and lock
the place up. Jimmy is whistling away to himself.*

JIMMY

That was a lot of fun, I've never done that before.

BILL

You're not wrong about that. I can't remember ever kicking the ball that
long.

JIMMY

Me neither.

BILL

It was sort of like being someone else for a time ... you know what I mean?

JIMMY

Like pretending to be a star player or something?

BILL

Not really. But something like that. I can't explain it!

JIMMY

Don't worry about it then.

BILL

Yeh! I guess so!

JIMMY

Say, do ya want me to show ya where I used to live? It's just three blocks
away.

BILL

Yeah sure.

34. INT BILL'S CAR

BILL

I thought you played a bit of footy?

JIMMY

Nah, just messed about really with me cousin when I stayed with him in
Perth about ten years back. That was a great time.

BILL

You know where the goals are, that's for sure.

JIMMY

Yeah, it's easy doing kick to kick, not like in a real game eh? But the goals
did feel sort of natural like, know what I mean?

BILL

Sure do! Are we nearly there?

JIMMY

Just take the next street to the left, and it's a few doors down from the
corner.

*They seem very comfortable in each other's company. They
both seem very happy and contented with themselves as
Jimmy points down the street to a house.*

35. EXT HOUSE   **MOMENTS LATER**

JIMMY

(Pointing to the house)
There it is, the one with the red brick fence. I built it meself!

BILL

(incredulously)
Really? Isn't it a bit old for you?

JIMMY

(looking confused)
What do ya mean?

A girl in her twenties is out washing her new car as Bill's car pulls up outside. She looks up at the two guys and is a bit surprised when Jimmy gets out and starts patting the brickwork. He starts to whistle.

ROSE MURPHY

Can I help you?

JIMMY

Nah I'm sweet, just admiring the fancy brickwork.

ROSE

Oh yeah! Right!

BILL

(getting out of the car)
No it's OK really, he used to live here.

ROSE

No he didn't!

JIMMY

(turning to face Bill)
I lived here all right! Built this bloody fence meself!

ROSE

What's going on here? I don't know you or him and neither of you lived here! I'll guarantee you of that! Oh and the fence was built by my granddad! Planning to rob us are you?

She grins at both of them, as her two brothers lob up to check the commotion. One of them recognizes Bill as his teacher, and Bill talks to him.

BILL

Is it true what she said?
(The boy nods)
We must have made a mistake. See you tomorrow at school.

With Jimmy protesting profusely they drive off looking very bewildered.

---

36. INT OFFICE SETTING   **10PM SUNDAY**

It is a modern office scene, and we see two men go through a door that is signed "President". One of them goes behind a big desk, while the other sits in a chair facing him.

COMMITTEE MAN

Did you hear what happened to Poss?

COACH

No I didn't...

COMMITTEE MAN

Stroke, Frank!

COACH

Blimey! Is she OK?

COMMITTEE MAN

Not too bad, I saw her yesterday for a few minutes.

COACH

I know you think I've done my dash don't you? But I reckon if we can stir the boys with some good old club pride, they'll do fine.

COMMITTEE MAN

And Frank, how do you intend to do it now, seeing as four of our top boys have already signed with other clubs for next season?

COACH

I know! But I reckon if we go back to the old ground, and give 'em a taste of where we all started, it might shake their trees a bit. What do ya reckon?

COMMITTEE MAN

Well it might be just as well, the way the sponsors are talking. We'll probably be back there anyway next season the way things are.

COACH

So if Thursday at four is OK with you then?

COMMITTEE MAN

Yeah! OK Frank, we can give it a whirl! Nothing to lose at this moment!

---

37. INT THE DELI   **3.45PM TUESDAY**

Ken is working cleaning the counter. He looks up to see Bill and Jimmy turn up to open the grounds.

KEN

Would it be alright missus if I go early tonight?

COUNTER LADY

Yeah that's OK, no-one here anyway.

KEN

(very happy already half way out the door)
Thanks! Yeah, See ya then!

---

38. EXT THE OLD GROUND   **MOMENTS LATER**

Ken wanders over to Bill and Jimmy. Bill looks pleased to see him.

KEN

Hi guys, ya mind if I join in for a kick?

BILL

Hi Ken, this is Jimmy, come on and tog up.

Jimmy and Ken eye each other off

KEN

We met before, yeah, didn't we?

BILL

'course you did! Forgot all about it already.

*They are seen training hard, with Ken running very swiftly
and all three boys kicking extremely well.*

JIMMY

(yelling out to Ken)
Pass the ball over here! Good kick!

*After the training session, the boys are diligently cleaning
the balls and their boots.*

BILL

(Looking casually over at Ken)
Every Tuesday and Thursday at four. OK?

KEN

Gee thanks! Yeah I'll be there!

BILL

Ken, why don't you arrange with your boss so that you don't have a drama
each time? Maybe do a bit extra on some other days.

KEN

Yeah! I'll do that! Ya got my word on it! Yeah! See yous Thursday!

JIMMY

See yous then.

BILL

See you later.

---

39. EXT THE OLD GROUND   **THURSDAY AROUND 3:30**

---

*Ken notices a big bus pull up outside the ground and a lot
of people start milling around the entrance. Pretty soon,
Bill and Jimmy drive up and open the gates. Ken goes
across to join them.*

JIMMY

What's going on?

BILL

It's training day, mate!

OFFICIAL 1

I thought Poss would be here to open up for us.

BILL

She's had a bit of a stroke, asked me to keep the grounds open. We also
train here as well. If that's OK with you?

OFFICIAL 1

A stroke! No-one ever tells me nothing around here!

BILL

Yeah! She's over the worst of it.

OFFICIAL 1

We all gotta get old don't we? I'll look in on her sometime.

BILL

She'd like that. What about us training?

OFFICIAL 2

Yeah, that would be alright, just don't interfere with the boys or the coach.

BILL

No worries! I'll lock up after you all have finished.

Bill, Jimmy and Ken are doing laps during their warm up session as the club's team runs out onto the ground. Bill goes into the goal square down one end of the oval while Jimmy and Ken take turns in belting the ball through the goal posts. Some of the officials have already taken some notice of the talent out there and forget about watching their own team in lieu of observing the three amateurs.

One of Bill's kick-outs goes over both the other two's heads and Ken gives chase. As the ball is very close to some of the club team, some of their players break rank to run the ball down, but Ken is much too fast for them, and easily eludes their efforts as he scoops up the ball and delivers a perfect pass to Jimmy who had led out to the boundary line, about 60 meters from the goal. Ken has an amazed look on his face over what he just did.

Effortlessly, Jimmy turns and fires the ball over Bill's head through for a goal. The officials applaud madly much to the displeasure of the coach and other players.

When Bill, Jimmy and Ken finish their session, the two officials come down to chat with them. A group of spirits are also watching quietly.

OFFICIAL 1

That was pretty impressive, what club do you boys play for?

KEN

We don't play for no-one except ourselves.
(He laughs wildly)

OFFICIAL 2

No-one plays that well without playing somewhere!

BILL

It's true though, we're really only here to help out Poss.

OFFICIAL 2

Are you boys interested in playing for this club?

BILL

Hadn't really thought too much about it. You're not that desperate?
Maybe you are at that! What are you offering?

OFFICIAL 2

I'll have to clear it with the coach, but we couldn't do any worse than try
you three boys out on Saturday's match at Prince's Park. How does that
sound?

BILL

Could be fun, what about it guys?

*They all nod with heaps of smiles as the two officials go off
and chat with the coach and then bring him over to meet
the boys.*

COACH

Training is not match practice! But I seen what you were doing out there,
and it's OK with me for Saturday, because there are these three turkeys
that I'll have a lot of pleasure in dropping. Fill out the forms and I'll see
you at one on Saturday! Well done! You made the team, if you could call it
that.

BILL

Thanks coach, we'll give you all we have!

JIMMY

What about regular stuff and all that?

OFFICIAL 1

I'll take care of you, and you'll have some dollars in your pockets to boot!

JIMMY

That's sweet! Now ya're talking!

---

40. INT PRINCE'S PARK CHANGE ROOM   **SATURDAY 2PM**

*Cut to match day where Bill, Jimmy and Ken are formally
introduced to the other team members. There are a lot of
disconsolate guys there and they vent their feelings only to
be quietened down by the coach. The three spirits are also
there watching.*

COACH

There's a few changes to the team today boys, so check your new
positions! And we have a few new faces here as well, so make them
welcome!

MAC

(looking directly at Ken)
What are these blokes doing here? Where's Smithy and Greggo? I don't
play with bloody bungs.

Bill gets in between the player's eye and Ken, sees that Ken is getting very red in the face and obviously uncomfortable.

BILL
(Getting angry)
Listen mate, just watch your mouth! Who the hell do you think you are?
(looking back at Ken)
You OK?

KEN
Yeah I'm alright, I'm used to it.

BILL
(Getting angrier)
You shouldn't have to be!

KEN
(Proudly)
It's OK.
(looking back at Mac)
Didn't we come here to play footy?

COACH
Come on guys, give 'em a chance, it's only one game!

A lot of grunting of alright and they all run out onto the field.

41. EXT PRINCE'S PARK FIELD

The opening minutes are a torrid affair with Bill and Ken shining through it. Suddenly the ball is in the air on the half forward flank and Jimmy takes a spectacular mark. A player's first kick in the majors is a special event and Jimmy, to the roar of the crowd, boots home a goal. All the players run over and pat him on the back and shake hands. At the end of the first quarter, he has got 4 goals and had a hand in 2 others. The second quarter seems to be a repeat of the first with the club up by about 6 goals.

MAC
(Looking directly at Ken)
You guys are OK! We can win this one!

JIMMY
Just keep kicking the ball to me, and we'll be sweet!

The radio announcers are having a field day with the new players doing so well and are really hyping up the whole affair. We see many more typical footy scenes and the final score has the club winning by a big margin. Everybody is ecstatic, including the sponsors who make their way up to Jimmy to congratulate him. Before leaving the field an opposition Aboriginal player, Wally, comes up to Ken and shakes his hand.

WALLY

Good game, brother! Where you from?

KEN

(Happy, muddied and a bit of blood coming from a gash over his right eye)

Thanks, Yeah, I was born near here. Wathaurong!

WALLY

Oh yeah! I'm from up Bendigo way. Me name is Wally! Do you want to come and have some dinner with us tonight?

KEN

Thanks Wally but I can't tonight, I sort of promised these blokes, yeah, for our break-up. I work at the café near the old ground. Let's do it another time?

WALLY

Ok! See ya!

Wally runs off with his team as players and officials mill around Ken while they walk off the ground to the cheers of the home crowd.

---

42. INT CHANGE ROOMS   **MOMENTS LATER**

SPONSOR 1

(Patting Jimmy on the back and beaming from ear to ear)

Not too many players have done what you just did. 10 goals in your first game, bloody magnificent! What do you do for a quid when you're not kicking goals?

JIMMY

Actually, I'm looking for a job, used to be ….

SPONSOR 1

You got a job now my boy, here's my card, come and see me on Monday, that is if you're going to stay with the club next season.

JIMMY

Gee thanks, that'll be sweet! Yeah we'll all be here, won't we guys?

General mumbles of yes

A trainer comes over with a band-aid for Ken's gash

TRAINER

There you go. You know you remind me of someone!

KEN

Yeah, who's that? Thanks for the band-aid!

TRAINER

That's OK, played a good game today.

KEN

Who'd I remind ya of?

TRAINER

Dunno! But it'll come to me.
(They both laugh, as Jimmy and Bill come over)
You guys did us proud today! Good on ya!

JIMMY AND BILL

Thanks mate.

---

43. INT. OFFICE SETTING **SAME TIME**

*Two men in suits, the well-dressed man and his associate
are discussing the game.*

ASSOCIATE

That insurance policy only has another three weeks, you know.

WELL DRESSED MAN

I know. I've taken care of it, sort of.

ASSOCIATE

What do you mean Alan?

WELL DRESSED MAN

Well the fella I got to do the job, was the same fella who kicked ten goals
for us this afternoon.

ASSOCIATE

How the hell did that happen?

WELL DRESSED MAN

I don't know! He was a homeless bum, sleeping in the old club when I
made him the offer.

ASSOCIATE

And you never knew he was a footballer?

WELL DRESSED MAN

I'm telling you, he was a nobody! He took my money, promised to do the
job by next week ... and then there he is.

ASSOCIATE

Listen! We could all be in a lot of hot water if that insurance money
doesn't come through. There's a lot at stake here ... just fix it for sure, with
or without that fella, see!

WELL DRESSED MAN

OK! OK! I'll fix it!

ASSOCIATE

You better!

---

44. IN HOTEL BREAK UP DINNER **SAME NIGHT**

*We see a lot of couples going through the hotel into the
function room, amongst them is the girl from the fence
scene, holding onto an older woman. Bill, Jimmy and Ken*

walk in, dressed in smart casual clothes and plenty of people come over to them as they find their table to sit down.

GUEST
(speaking to Bill)
That was my old number you were wearing today, and I don't think it's seen a more honest game than the one you just played.

BILL
Thanks for that, I know I'll sleep well tonight!

Everyone laughs

JIMMY
Won't we all!

The girl from the fence comes over and looks at Jimmy, and he takes an immediate interest.

JIMMY (cont'd)
Well hello again.

ROSE
(holding out her hand)
We didn't really get introduced last time did we? My name is Rose, Rose Murphy.

JIMMY
(a little taken aback by her presence)
That's a lovely name.

ROSE
You're Jimmy Rivers aren't you?

JIMMY
That's me all right. What yous doing here?

ROSE
Family tradition you could say. My gran is always invited, and I thought it might be fun to see you again.

She laughs out loud and everyone turns to look at them.

ROSE (cont'd)
You played a great game today, did the jumper proud.

JIMMY
It's been a big day all 'round for me. Would yous like to join us?

ROSE
I'll ask my gran. Wait here, I'll be back in a jiff.

JIMMY
I'll come with ya!

Jimmy gets up and walks with Rose to where her gran is sitting talking to some friends.

GRAN

The way that young man led out to the pocket and then made the goals look so easy. It was almost the way I remember my Garry doing it.

She stops short as she sees Rose and Jimmy come over.

GRAN (cont'd)

That's the fella!

ROSE

Gran, I'd like you to meet Jimmy. Jimmy this is my gran.

When both Jimmy and gran look each other in the eye they both appear to get teary and Jimmy grabs her hand very tightly as they are introduced.

JIMMY

(wiping his eyes)
Nice to meet ya.
Yous look so familiar to me. Me mother died recently. Maybe that's it.

GRAN

I know what it's like to lose someone.

ROSE

Is it OK if I sit with Jimmy, Gran?

GRAN

You go ahead. He looks like a nice boy, have some fun dear.

ROSE

Sounds like some good instructions! Let's go!

GRAN

(watching as they both waltz away)
He even walks like Garry. Oh my! I still miss him.

The well-dressed man spots Jimmy and taps him on the shoulder.

WELL DRESSED MAN

Excuse me love, could I have a word in your young man's ear.

ROSE

Hi Alan! OK but deliver him back to me safe and sound!

WELL DRESSED MAN

Five minutes, Rose.

Rose goes over to where Bill and Ken are sitting.

WELL DRESSED MAN (cont'd)

What sort of game are you playing here son?

JIMMY RIVERS

I know! I'll do it, 'cause I said I would... but...

WELL DRESSED MAN

Just do it! Don't double cross me son! You'll be in jail quicker than you can click your fuckin' fingers! Get my drift?

JIMMY RIVERS

OK! OK!

MONTAGE: Various shots of merriment with all the characters enjoying themselves. Jimmy and Rose do a bit of dancing. A few speeches mentioning that Frank, the coach, has been re-appointed for a further year, and that the team would be training at the old ground from now on. Everyone clapping and applauding.

MC

And now the moment you've all been waiting for . . .best and fairest for the last game! One vote to Bill Watson on the half back flank

The MC's announcements are copntinually interspersed with loud clapping and cheering.

MC (cont'd)

two votes to Ken Merryman,

Ken nods, beaming from ear to ear.

MC (cont'd)

... a great game on the ball and of course best on the ground by a country mile. Jimmy Rivers! Well done son, best game at full forward that I've ever seen at the club. Those votes didn't do a thing to change the leader board and the award for this year goes to Jack Ross again, second year in a row! Come on up here and accept the trophy, you know what to do.

JACK ROSS

Thanks guys! Great game today eh? We showed 'em how good we could be when we played liked a team! Can't wait for next season!

MC

Well it's back to some old style dancing now, so take your partners for "The Pride of Erin".

ROSE

(to Jimmy)

Not with me Fred Astaire! Why don't you ask Gran to dance with you? Go on!

JIMMY

Ok I will!

Jimmy goes over to Gran and holds out his hand and she quietly goes with him, and they dance together to the amazement of Rose and everyone else.

JIMMY (cont'd)

Ya dance real well Gran.

GRAN

Well it was my favourite dance, but I haven't done it for a lot of years.

JIMMY

Well yous haven't forgot any of the steps.

GRAN

(a tear trickling down her face)
No, some things I'll always remember. Thanks for asking me son.

JIMMY

(also a bit flushed)
You're very welcome.

*The night blends away with a montage of shots of everyone
in a very happy frame of mind. A few independent close-ups
of Gran and Jimmy show them to be somewhat distracted
from time to time during conversations with friends.*

45. INT. THE OLD GROUND   SUNDAY NIGHT

*Jimmy carries a flashlight and a can of petrol. He starts to
splash the petrol around the floor. Suddenly he stops and
gazes at the old photos on the wall.*

*The spirits are now all around him watching as he forgets
his task and runs out into the night.*

ERIC

Good boy! Keep talking to him Garry.

Garry

I'll try.

46. EXT. UNDER A STREET LIGHT

JIMMY

(speaking on his mobile)
I'm not doing it!

ALAN

(off screen through phone)
You bastard! You gave me your word!

JIMMY

I know! But I'm not doing it, if yous do it, I'll dob ya!

ALAN

So now you're the town hero and toughie, is that it? Well let me tell you,
you're as good as dead mate!

Jimmy turns off his phone and sprints away into the night.

Jimmy walks in to a somewhat crowded station.

POLICEMAN
Take a seat son and I'll be with you in about ten minutes, Ok?

Jimmy nods and sits near a scruffy boy of about fourteen.

BOY
What you in for?

JIMMY RIVERS
Helping a mate! What about you?

BOY
I got caught see, chucking a stone through the school window, say aren't
you the footy player?

JIMMY RIVERS
Yeah! Did yous go to the game then?

BOY
Bloody great game eh? You kicked twelve yourself!

JIMMY RIVERS
It was only ten, a lot of fun, eh?

BOY
I'll say!

JIMMY RIVERS
Did yous ever think about the students in the school who are trying to get
on, the broken glass and damage and all?

BOY
Oh they'll be alright.

JIMMY RIVERS
Yeah, but is it fair that yous do that to them, is it fair?

BOY
I suppose not...

JIMMY RIVERS
Then why did yous do it?

BOY
It wasn't just me!

JIMMY RIVERS
I know.

BOY
Nobody takes any time to play with us, so what do you expect!

JIMMY RIVERS
Can you kick a footy?

BOY

'Course!

JIMMY RIVERS

Well write me number on your phone and give me a call on Tuesday
around four.

BOY

You mean it?

JIMMY RIVERS

I said so didn't I!

BOY

Yeah, what's the catch?

JIMMY RIVERS

Only if yous can stay out of trouble. Deal?

BOY

Gee thanks! Wow!

POLICEMAN

(calling from the counter)
Jimmy Rivers!

JIMMY RIVERS

I'll see yous later!

JIMMY RIVERS (cont'd)

I need to talk to someone, private like, is that possible?

PolICEMAN

You're the footballer from Saturday?

JIMMY RIVERS

Yeah, hell it was only one game and everyone knows me like!

POLICEMAN

It was some game! I'll get the sergeant, come with me.

Jimmy goes with the policeman

SERGEANT

What can I do for you son?

POLICEMAN

This is the fella I was telling you about Merv ...

SERGEANT

That'll do John, just shut the door on your way out will you.

SERGEANT (cont'd)

I'm all ears.

JIMMY RIVERS

Some bloke, Alan I think his name is. Big shot around the club...

SERGEANT

Alan Tomlinson?

JIMMY RIVERS

Don't know his surname.

SERGEANT

(pointing at an article in the newspaper)
This the chap?

JIMMY RIVERS

Yeah, that's him!

SERGEANT

Councillor Alan Tomlinson, what about him.

*The young boy gazes at the front counter. The spirits of Eric
and Garry are also wandering around.*

JIMMY RIVERS

...... yous got to stop him. I know I took his money, see. Lock me up if yous
like, but I don't want the club burning on me conscience!

SERGEANT

I'll have a word with him. Don't you go leaving town.

JIMMY RIVERS

I'm not going anywhere.

SERGEANT

Good! Just keep your nose clean from now on and all will be well, I
promise you.

JIMMY RIVERS

Thanks sergeant!

SERGEANT

Go on, get out of here!

*Jimmy leaves the room and winks at the young boy as he
leaves the building.*

ERIC

You got your work ahead of you with this fella.

GARRY

We'll be fine, you'll see.

ERIC

I guess I will.

---

48. EXT/INT MONTAGE OF VARIOUS SHOTS OVER A PERIOD OF SIX MONTHS

*Pre season training is suddenly upon the team and we see
Bill visiting Poss during her recovery as well as Jimmy in his
new job and new relationship with Rose, Ken enjoying his
new status.*

COACH

This is it boys, and you know I'm still here by the skin of me teeth. Do it for the club this season, let's show 'em all what we're made of. And have some pride in yourselves for a change! You've earned it! It's been a hard run and we're as fit as Mallee bulls! But one last thing! I don't want to lose any home games, and that means today as well!
(shouting)
We don't lose here this season!

50.   **MONTAGE OF SEVERAL MATCHES**

Various footy scenes with the scoreboard showing the team coming out on top from the first game.

Romance blossoms between Rose and Jimmy, as she screams when he kicks a goal.

Game after game the club does well. Much of the focus of shots is on Bill, Jimmy and Ken marking and kicking goal after goal.

RADIO COMMENTATOR1

Here we go again! Jimmy Rivers! He owns the ball today!

RADIO COMMENTATOR 2

Look at that ball go!

RADIO COMMENTATOR 1

Have you ever seen anyone like him before, playing for this club.

RADIO COMMENTATOR 2

He's a right gem! He's the real McCoy all right!

51.   **EXT A STREET IN THE SUBURBS**   **10PM**

We cut to a few weeks later where Ken has just been to the pictures with his girlfriend Rita, it's a Saturday night, wet and cold, he notices Wally, the Aboriginal player from the other team that he'd met earlier, swaggering down the opposite side of the street, with some blood over his lips and eyes glazed. Ken tells Rita to stay where she is, and he goes over towards Wally.

KEN
(calling out as he approaches Wally)
Hey Wally!
(no response)
Hey Wally, it's me, Ken! Brother, what happened to ya?

WALLY
(drunkenly, slurring his speech)
Got a smoke mate?

KEN

What happened to ya?

WALLY

Let's go get a drink, brother?

KEN

Come home with me Wally and we'll get ya cleaned up? How's that sound?

WALLY

(getting angry and not really recognizing Ken)
I want a bloody drink, you all the same! Fuckin' piss off then! Can you lend me a quid then?

KEN

No brother, you've had enough eh?

WALLY

Let go of me!

KEN

(taking Wally's hand in a compassionate but firm manner)
It's me, Ken! And I'm taking ya home whether ya like it or not! Don't ya recognize me, brother?

WALLY

(slowly coming to his senses)
Hey brother, good to see ya!

KEN

(Calling out to Rita)
It's OK now, can ya help me get him home?

RITA

(crossing over the street to join them)
Of course I can! Is he a friend of yours?

KEN

Sort of! I know where he's at! It's bloody tough some times, ya know what I mean?

RITA

Then let's get him home, eh!

Ken, Rita and Wally amble off together under the most disapproving eyes of a few local residents.

KEN

What do they know about anything! Come on let's get him off the streets before the coppers come.

---

52. INT KEN'S HOME   **SUNDAY AM**

It's 10am on the Sunday morning, Ken is making coffee and Wally comes waltzing in to the kitchen, not knowing where he is.

KEN

Big night eh?

WALLY

Yeah! Hey I know ya! How ya doing brother?

KEN

Not bad Wally, you're the one with the cut lip and all.

WALLY

Yeah, I copped a beauty from this bloke. He didn't hurt me! I got a couple
in as well.

KEN

Yeah yeah!

WALLY

Where did we meet up?

KEN

The main street. Couldn't leave ya in the gutter, could I?

WALLY

(sadly, thoughtfully.)
I belong there don't I? Every bloody weekend after the game, it all goes
bad for me! These white boys make me do things and then laugh at me!
And I bloody well do them, don't I?

KEN

(compassionately)
I know! I've been there too!

WALLY

(frustrated)
What can I do? Ya tell me?

KEN

I don't know. But it seems to me that ya got a choice in what ya do, don't
ya? And these blokes are not really your mates if they're laughing at ya. So,
choose not to do what they say, and see if it works out a bit better. Can't
be worse for ya!

WALLY

Yeah, easier said than done.

KEN

Want a coffee?

*Wally and Ken spend the day together watching TV and
kicking a ball in the backyard. At about 6pm Wally decides
to go home.*

WALLY

I had a good day brother, thanks for your wisdom. I'll remember it.

KEN

(laughing)

Ya better! We're playing your mob next week aren't we? So I'll see ya then.

WALLY

Yeah, Ya guys are doing alright this year! See ya later!

KEN

See ya!

---

53. EXT THE FOOTBALL GROUND   **TUESDAY 4PM**

> *Ken sees Bill and Jimmy drive up, and he races out to meet them from the café. They all react as good mates do. Some other players start to roll up for training as well and everyone is on a high, as they go inside to tog up for the session.*

---

54. INT THE CLUB ROOMS

KEN

(speaking softly to Bill)

I got this mate who needs a bit of guidance sort of.

BILL

Do you want me to have a chat to him?

KEN

Would ya?

BILL

Yeah sure, just bring him around and we can talk it through.

KEN

Thanks Bill. I mean that.

BILL

Anytime. Now let's get out there and do some laps. I'll race you!

(laughs wildly)

> *They both run through the doorway down the tunnel onto the ground, Jimmy not far behind them.*

JIMMY

Wait for me!

---

55. INT ROSE AND GRAN'S   **FRIDAY 7PM**

> *Rose's two brothers have sat very quietly through dinner, looking very admirably at Jimmy and nodding to him every now and then. Gran had put on a good meal and had placed a bottle of beer in easy reach of Jimmy.*

ROSE

(pushing the beer away from Jimmy)

You got a game tomorrow, haven't you?

JIMMY

How come you're always right?

ROSE

I'm a woman!

Everyone laughs.

ROSE (cont'd)

You remember when you first came here, you said you built the fence.

GRAN

What was that about Garry's fence?

ROSE

Oh nothing Gran, just Jimmy got the houses mixed up a while back, and thought this was his place.

JIMMY

(looking a bit puzzled by it all)
It's strange isn't it? I've never built a fence, and yet it just felt as if I had.
(trying to laugh it off)
Must have been in another life.

GRAN

(sighing)
Garry once told me that that fence would last longer than all of us. He was right! Even your mum, Rose, would sit for hours on it as if it might bring him back. And now she's with him too.

JIMMY

All that effort in making those bricks himself, would make any man proud.

GRAN

(looking a little shocked)
How could you possibly have known that?

JIMMY

I don't know! Am I right?

GRAN

Yes, they were hard times in those days and there were no bricks around, not that we could have afforded them new. So Garry and his best mate Merv Owens, decided to make their own in Merv's back yard. It was a messy affair I can tell you, but they did it! They did it!

Everyone starts to pack up the plates and put them in the sink for washing.

GRAN (cont'd)

You all go out and have some fun, I'll do the dishes. Go on!

ROSE

(kissing Gran on the cheek)
Thanks Gran. Come on Jimmy. See you later.

Jimmy looks a little strange as he slowly gets up from the table

JIMMY
(becoming weepy)
I'm very happy yous invited me here tonight Gran. But I've got to say that I'm also very sad. See, I can't help meself!

Rose goes over to Jimmy and gives him a big hug, while the others there watch on in some amazement.

ROSE
That's Ok darling.

JIMMY
I love yous Rose, and I want to marry yous, but.

GRAN
What is it son?

JIMMY
I don't know how to say this, so that yous all don't run a country mile from me. But I do need to talk it out.

GRAN
Just say what's on your mind son, and we'll listen to you.

ROSE
It'll be OK.

JIMMY
(sighing)
OK
It's just that for the past couple of months I've been getting these thoughts. About this house, and a whistling tune that's driving me crazy. Because it's so familiar and yet I don't even know it.

ROSE
Whistle it to me and maybe I will recognise it.

He whistles the tune, Rose looks blankly on, but Gran's eyes fill with tears.

ROSE (cont'd)
Gran, are you OK?

GRAN
That was our favourite tune! Garry would whistle it everywhere! What are you up to son?

JIMMY
I wish I knew. But when yous spoke of Merv Owens, I got a flash image of two soldiers, one with bright red hair.

GRAN
(getting very upset)
Stop! Please don't do this to me!

ROSE

What are you talking about?

GRAN

Merv had red hair!

ROSE

(getting very interested in the story)
You said two soldiers! What was the other one like?

JIMMY

(to Gran)
I do need to talk about this, please, because I think I'm going crazy, and it's
killing me.

GRAN

I don't know if I want to hear it. But go on.

JIMMY

Well, the other chap is helping the red haired guy, who looks pretty sick,
through a trench somewhere.

GRAN

Oh my!

JIMMY

The guy just whistles that tune and every now and then says to his mate
"hang on Kicker, you'll be right". What does it all mean?

GRAN

(collapsing into a chair)
Garry always called Merv, Kicker, they were best mates.

Gran begins to sob. Rose goes over to comfort her.

ROSE

(turning to Jimmy)
How do you know these things?

JIMMY

I don't know! But somehow I feel a lot better by sharing it with yous. I still
don't understand it all.

ROSE

Gran, whatever happened to Merv Owens, is he still around?

GRAN

No dear, they both died out there. It must have been terrible! But at least
they had each other, and that's a comfort.

JIMMY

I'm sorry Gran, for telling yous this story, it's …

GRAN

It's not your fault son, I felt something too between us at the club break
up. But how strange it is for me to have these feelings again after all this
time!

JIMMY

I better get some sleep, it's been a long day for me. Goodnight and thanks for everything.

(tturning to Rose)

If yous want me, like I want you, yous better pick a date. Let's not waste any precious time! Do yous love me?

ROSE

(excitedly moving over to Jimmy)

Are you crazy? No! I didn't mean that!

They all laugh.

ROSE (cont'd)

'Course I do!

She hugs him and they kiss.

GRAN

That settles it then, doesn't it?

The two brothers come over and one kisses Rose while the other pats Jimmy on the back as the scene fades out.

---

56. INT. CLUB ROOM   **BEFORE THE GAME**

Cut to the club room, it is half an hour before the main game, and the coach is addressing the team and discussing player positions using a big white-board.

COACH

OK guys, there are no changes to last week's team, you'll be happy to hear, we're not going to break a winning combination, are we? So let's do it again!

The coach notices Bill looking a little disappointed and down, so he looks in his direction.

COACH (cont'd)

What's up Bill?

BILL

Coach, I was thinking of a few things. Is it alright?

COACH

Sure, go ahead!

BILL

OK, I feel Tommy and Bruce have not had enough on the field time, and if we leave them on the bench week in week out, then down the track it's going to rebound pretty heavily on us.

At this, the players grunt some positive things amongst themselves.

COACH

What did you have in mind?

BILL

Maybe Steve and I could sit on the bench for this one, and put Bruce on the flank in my spot, and run Tommy out of a forward pocket, and see how it goes. What do you think?

COACH

That'll weaken our defence!

BILL

(turning to the two players)
I reckon these guys will rise to the occasion, and do the job, won't you?

A lot of shouting and grunting of the players approval eg "yeah!" and "great idea!"

COACH

OK. That'll do! Settle down! Good idea Bill, that's what we'll do then. Anyone else got any pearls of wisdom to share with us? OK then let's kill this mob!

Lots of yelling as the team runs out onto the field to the wild applause of the many fans.

---

57. EXT THE GROUND   **MID AFTERNOON**

Ken says hi to Wally, from the other team on the ground, and Jimmy searches for Rose in the stands, and then smiles when he catches her eye.

Montage of football action scenes for the first quarter with a home team player being carried off the field on a stretcher after a heavy collision. Steve runs onto the ground and the coach comes down to check on the injured player and then sits with Bill on the bench.

COACH

He should be OK for next week, just a bit of concussion.

BILL

That's good! See how he feels on Tuesday, but even giving him a week's break might be better too!

COACH

Yeah, we'll see.

Montage: Jimmy is starring at Full Forward with some great goals and by half time, both teams are about even. At half time the players come inside for the break; they shake Bill's hand appreciatively and pat him on the back..

Montage: There are more footy scenes, including Bill getting a run in the last quarter. The team wins by two goals. Everyone is ecstatic over the hard fought match.

JIMMY
(to Bill and Ken)
Big news guys! Rosie and me's gonna get hitched. Engagement arty's at her joint tonight. 6.30.

BILL
Congrats mate. Ken and I'll be there.

KEN
(whispering to Bill)
Bill, do you think you could join me for a drink at the cafe after the game.

BILL
Yeah sure!

KEN
Are you sure?

BILL
That'd be alright. We can then go to Jimmy and Rose's together. How's that sound?

KEN
Thanks Bill, I'd like that a lot.

The players shower and change, and we see Jimmy rush out to meet Rose. Ken and Bill stroll out with their bags slung over their backs. A couple of girls make a pass at both of them, to which they both politely decline. We see them cross the road to the café and go inside.

59. INT CAFÉ   **LATE AFTERNOON**

Ken looks nervously around but can't see Wally. Suddenly Wally comes swaggering through the door.

KEN
Hey Wally, over here!

Wally comes over, also carrying his sports bag and smiles as he walks towards them.

WALLY
G'day brother, g'day mate.

KEN
This is Bill.

BILL
G'day.

WALLY
You guys seem to have the wood on us alright! Great game though.

BILL
(laughing)
You played pretty well yourself today. I was watching from the bench for
most of the match.

WALLY
I noticed.

KEN
I asked Bill to join us for a chat, you don't mind do ya?

WALLY
What about?

KEN
You know, all the shit you been getting into.

WALLY
Oh that.

BILL
I can imagine how tough it must be for you guys. Our team is not filled
with saints either.

WALLY
Yeah! So what can I do? Nobody really listens to me!

BILL
Stand proud to who you are. You don't have to act white just to prove
something or please someone.

WALLY
Yeah yeah!

BILL
You'll get more respect in the long run by not reacting in their way. Know
what I mean?

WALLY
Yeah!

BILL
It's your call, you choose. But there'll be no slagging from our boys when
I'm around.

KEN
That's right Wally, Bill stood up for me and those blokes just sort of accept
me, I didn't have to do anything.

BILL
You don't have to be friends with everyone! Hell it's hard enough with the
real thing sometimes.

WALLY
I don't know if I can do it! But it's the first time I ever spoke to one of you
guys that didn't want something off me. Thanks!

Ken gives Wally a hug.

KEN
He's OK isn't he?

WALLY
Yeah, and you're pretty lucky to be his friend.

KEN
I know.

60. INT GRAN'S HOUSE   **6PM**

*The scene fades in to the engagement party where Bill,
Ken and Rita are seen mingling with the crowd there. Gran
is seen grabbing Jimmy from the crowd and leading him to
her bedroom. Pictures of her late husband Garry in uniform
and in footy gear, are on the dresser.*

GRAN
(very nervously)
I can't stop thinking about what you said last night son. It's almost too
unbelievable to believe! But I want to believe!

JIMMY
(very measured)
I know! How do yous think I feel about it?

GRAN
(tenderly)
It's almost like he's trying to send me a message.

JIMMY
I think he is.

GRAN
What do you mean?

JIMMY
It's just a feeling, but I'm sure he was saying something like "it's not your
time yet Jess, you've got a job to do, I'll wait for yous"

GRAN
That's just the sort of thing he'd say. Thank you son..

She hugs him and whispers).

GRAN (cont'd)
I love you Garry, always have and always will.

*They walk back into the lounge and Rose comes over to
them*

ROSE
(looking a bit concerned)
Where did you two get off to?

GRAN

(a bit flushed)

It was my fault dear.

JIMMY

(beaming)

If this isn't the best day of me life, so far.

ROSE

(also beaming)

Mine too.

Montage: There are more scenes of congratulatory conversation from various people to Jimmy and Rose, and through the noisy atmosphere we catch a glimpse of Gran with an inward smile of contentment on her face. Rita starts to get very affectionate with Ken, who returns the attention by putting his arm around her. Bill looks happy talking with the brothers of Rose and the scene fades out on a very happy household.

---

61. INT. HOSPITAL ROOM   **SUNDAY MORNING**

Bill and Poss are deep in conversation about the team.

BILL

We have been able to get the ball a lot easier from the ruck in the past two weeks.

POSS

I was listening to the wireless …. They love this Jimmy Rivers alright. I'd like to meet him one day.

BILL

He's a good mate! Just got engaged last night after the game, to Rose Murphy. Do you know her?

POSS

I've seen her around with her grandmother. That family, and others, is what makes this club so great, if you know what I mean?

BILL

Yeah! I sure do. I'll bring them around to meet you if you like?

POSS

I would like that, thanks.

BILL

What position did your man play?

POSS

On the ball, he roved for about 200 games.

BILL

Yeah!

POSS

In the good old days it was. We were an OK team then. Won a premiership and all!

BILL

That's our target too.

POSS

Stay focussed and it'll happen, you'll see.

BILL

We'll be trying alright.

They both smile at each other, as the nurse comes in to do her rounds.

BILL (cont'd)

I'll bring Jimmy by one day, better go now.

POSS

Yeah thanks, that'll be great! See ya!

BILL

See ya!

The nurse gives Bill a wry grin as he wanders out of the room, then smiles at Poss.

NURSE

He seems like a nice man.

POSS

He does doesn't he?

---

62. EXT. FOOTBALL GROUND   **TUESDAY 5PM**

During a break in training Bill talks with Jimmy and Ken).

BILL

That was bloody hard going!

KEN

I wonder how the bottom clubs train. I bet not this tough!

JIMMY

Yeah he's out to prove a point I reckon.

KEN

I'd say!

BILL

Say you know that old lady I've been seeing at the hospital?

JIMMY

Yeah!

BILL

Well her husband played over 200 games with this club.

JIMMY

Yeah?

BILL

Yeah! And she'd appreciate a visit from you two if you got the time after training?

KEN

It's OK with me. What about you Jimmy?

JIMMY

Yeah, it should be alright. Rose is going to meet me here so I suppose it'll be alright to bring her along too eh?

BILL

Can't see a problem. Looks like the coach has spotted us, let's get back at it.

Bill, Jimmy and Ken sprint off to the centre of the ground and are seen doing push-ups and stretches with the rest of the team.

---

63. INT CLUB ROOMS   6:30

After their showers, Rose joins them and Bill takes them all to the trophy room to show them a picture of the young husband of Poss.

BILL

(looking over at Jimmy)
You remember this room alright?

JIMMY

Sure do! Which one is he?

BILL

This one here in the '47 team, bottom row over there.

JIMMY

Oh yeah!

BILL

(noticing Ken not looking too well)
You OK mate?

KEN

Must be something about this room. I got to go for a crap or something,
(noticing Rose)
Oh sorry Rose.

ROSE

Oh that's OK! You go ahead, we'll wait for you.

Ken races off as Bill, Jimmy and Rose keep studying the old photographs, occasionally dusting them down as well.

Ken comes back, still a little shaky, and they drive in two cars to the hospital.

64. EXT HOSPITAL CAR PARK   6:45

A big sign indicates it is the Ballarat Rehabilitation Centre.

BILL
Poss is in room 2B. She'll be real happy!

They start to go through the doors, when Ken suddenly stops and turns back.

BILL (cont'd)
What's up mate?

KEN
Sorry mate, I'm not feeling the best. Do you think you could run me home?

BILL
Sure!
(to the other two)
You guys go in and I'll join you in twenty minutes.

JIMMY
OK! Hope yous feel better mate?

KEN
Thanks Jimmy, sorry Rose!

Bill and Ken drive off and Jimmy and Rose go back through the front door.

65. INT REHAB WARD

ROSE
That was a bit strange! I hope he will be alright?

JIMMY
Yeah! Bill will see him right, so don't yous worry too much.

ROSE
All the same, he looked like he'd seen a ghost or something!

They both burst out laughing as they make their way to Poss' room.

ROSE (cont'd)
Hi I'm Rose Murphy and you must be Poss, I presume?

POSS
I'm Poss alright, what can I do for you two?

ROSE
Oh it's just we are friends of Bill Watson and he asked me and Jimmy to come with him to visit with you.

POSS

So where is Bill?

ROSE

We had another friend of ours with us Ken Merryman and he took ill so Bill has driven him home.

POSS

Merryman you say. I once knew a Steve Merryman, I heard he died about ten years back. We were both Wathaurong. I'm the last from around this patch. I wonder if your mate was related. Sure like to know!

JIMMY

I'll ask him on Thursday at training.

POSS

You'd be Jimmy Rivers am I right?

JIMMY

Yeah! How'd yous know that?

POSS

I asked Bill to meet you. Looks like he is a man of his word eh?

JIMMY

Top bloke alright.

Jimmy, Poss and Rose are deep in conversation when Bill comes through the door.

POSS

No I never knew your grand dad, but we sure talked about him during my time. Your gran is a nice lady.
(noticing Bill by his bedside))
Oh there you are!

BILL

G'day! Had to …..

POSS

I know, Rose and Jimmy here told me.

BILL

I'm glad you guys are getting on OK.

ROSE

How's Kenny?

BILL

Strangely, he appears OK. As soon as we hit his place he chirped up and said he felt right as rain.

JIMMY

Yeah? He was like looking at death's door a minute ago!

BILL

Well he swears to me that there's two places he's not going into again.

POSS

What places are those?

BILL

The trophy room at the club and this hospital!
He is plumb scared of them and that's the plain truth! I was amazed
alright. He told me it must be something to do with his heritage, but it
beats me.

POSS

Do you know who his parents were?

BILL

No! He's been an orphan for as long as I've known him. Damn good kid
too.

POSS

Could you ask him if he knew a Steve Merryman? I'd sure appreciate it.

BILL

No problem! I'll let you know.

*They all chat on for about a half hour and then go their
separate ways. Rose and Jimmy go out for dinner and Bill
makes his way back to Ken's place to check up on him.*

66. INT KEN'S PLACE   **8PM**

---

*Ken lives in a little cottage by himself, and is just starting to
cook himself a big steak when Bill knocks on his door.*

KEN

Hi Bill what you doing here again?

BILL

Oh I was a bit worried about you. The way you were. Got a few minutes?

KEN

The steak's on and it's too big for me, so you can stay and have a bite and
keep me company if you like.

BILL

Best offer I've had all day.
You feeling OK now?

KEN

Yeah I'm alright. But I got this bad vibe that really threw me. It's gone now
though.

BILL

Old Poss was asking about a Steve Merryman. Is he related to you?

KEN

Yeah! He was my dad. Eleven years ago he died of a heart attack and all.

BILL

Sorry!

KEN

Oh that's OK, I miss him being here and guiding me, but I feel him everywhere if you know what I mean?

BILL

Sort of.

KEN

He was an elder of the Wathaurong. There were ten tribes in the early days around this region, and ours now is just me, I'm the last.

BILL

That's just what Poss said! She thought she was the last.

KEN

Yeah?

BILL

Well she would like to speak to you about it sometime.

KEN

OK I will! But I'm not going near that hospital! I reckon it'll have to wait till she gets out. How do you like your steak?

BILL

Red and walking!

Bill looks admiringly at Ken as they continue to chat.

67. EXT FOOTBALL GROUND   **3:30PM**

Montage: The scene fades into a football match in full swing. Ken gets knocked down in quite a vicious manner and is on the ground for a long time. While Bill and Jimmy make their way over to him, the player who had first spoken badly to Ken a year earlier, jumps to his defence and starts a brawl with the offending player. Ken notices what is happening, and looks very proud and privileged to being fought over, and especially by that player.

JIMMY

(concerned)
Yous OK mate?

KEN

(relieved to be OK after the knock)
I am now! Tell Mac to lay off the fighting! No use getting suspended with only two games to go eh?

JIMMY

(going over to Mac and pulling him off the other guy)
Come on Mac, only two games to go!

MAC

(all angrily fired up i)
Yeah but look what he did to Kenny!

JIMMY

Oh he's alright! He said to say thanks and all!

Mac and Ken lock eyes together and when Ken smiles at him, Mac goes over and yanks him up to his feet by his Guernsey

KEN

Thanks Mac!

MAC

You're welcome mate!

68. INT CLUB ROOMS   **LATER**

The sepia effect comes back over the scene. Bill, Ken and Jimmy are the last ones to leave the club rooms. Suddenly the three spirits leave the bodies of Bill, Ken and Jimmy and go floating down the corridors and then into the board room where all the photos are displayed.

69. INT. BOARD ROOM

All the spirits gather around Eric.

ERIC

Well I've got to say that in my humble opinion, the exercise went all right. What do you all think about it?

A lot of mumbles of agreement ensues

GARRY

Thanks Eric! And thanks fellas! It was wonderful! I always knew Jess would wait for me, and that our love was forever. But to be that close to her again!

PLAYER

We know what you mean! But the footy mate, you kicked some great goals!

EVERYONE

Yeah, yeah!

GARRY

That was great fun too! But you know, the last couple of games, well, I wasn't really doing anything! Jimmy is an OK lad!

EVERYONE

Yeah, yeah! What about now though?

GARRY

Oh, he'll be alright! I bet he won't even notice that I'm not there?

EVERYONE

I bet he does! I bet they all do! yeah, yeah!

ERIC

Well, the main thing was not really about winning games and kicking goals, even though it's a pretty good bonus. It was about the team playing and acting as a real team in all respects! Like the good old days! With good old fashioned values! And we did that, didn't we?

EVERYONE

Yeah, yeah!

They all laugh and clap and sing more of the club theme song, as the camera pans out and dissolves.

---

70. EXT TRAIN STATION   **SAME NIGHT**

Jimmy has a wild look in his eyes, and with his ruck-sack across his shoulders, waits for the train to Melbourne.

FAN

G'day Jimmy, where you off to?

JIMMY RIVERS

Can't yous give me a bloody minute to meself.

FAN

Sorry mate.... You're not doing a runner on us so close to the finals are you?

JIMMY RIVERS

What's it to ya anyway!

FAN

Just that you're the best thing that ever happened to this town, is all.

JIMMY RIVERS

Yeah! So what!

The train pulls in and Jimmy and the fan get on.

---

71. INT. TRAIN

JIMMY RIVERS

Fuckin' following me are yous?

FAN

I'm going to a funeral ... if you must know.

JIMMY RIVERS

Yeah, so?

FAN

Aren't you getting married?

JIMMY RIVERS

Look! What I do is me own business, see! So go sit somewhere else.

FAN

Ok, but I sure hope you work it all out.

JIMMY RIVERS
Yeah, yeah!

*The fan moves away and Jimmy is left deep in thought.
After a period of time, Jimmy gets off the train at a country
stop.*

---

72. EXT. HIGHWAY   **LATE AT NIGHT**

*Jimmy on the road hitching for a ride. A truck stops and he
gets in.*

---

73. EXT AWAY MATCH   **2:30PM**

The team is seen running onto the Bendigo Oval.

*Montage: More torrid footy scenes with Jimmy missing an
easy shot from thirty yards out, and in another sequence,
Bill gets caught holding the ball much to his disgust and
amazement, and in another sequence Ken kicks the ball
out of bounds on the full.*

Shots of the crowd looking shocked and disappointed.

---

74. EXT. PERIMETER OF OVAL FENCE

ROSE
(to Gran)
Can you believe that?

GRAN
He does look a little off his game today dear. I'm sure he'll be alright! I
remember Garry had a day like that when he couldn't kick 'em from ten
yards out directly in front one week, and the next week, he came out and
booted seven straight.

Gran chuckles loudly.

ROSE
I hope so! I didn't tell him, but a fella from the Carlton footy club rang me
yesterday looking for Jimmy.

GRAN
What did he want dear?

ROSE
He's heard about Jimmy see, and was going to watch a couple of games.

GRAN
(looking a little annoyed)
Why did he contact you dear, and not talk with Jimmy himself?

ROSE
I don't know!

GRAN

You make sure you tell Jimmy tonight! OK?

ROSE

I was going to!

---

75. INT. CLUB ROOMS   **AFTER GAME**

*The team has suffered its first loss of the season and the
coach is berating the players after the game.*

COACH

Our first loss boys! I'm a bit in shock Jimmy. I can't believe your game son,
where are you!

JIMMY

Sorry guys!

COACH

Steve, you played a blinder! Good boy! Best game all season! As for the
rest of you's! Well it's best we forget this game and concentrate on next
week! It's our last match at home! And you all know what that means!

EVERYONE

(yelling wildly)
We don't lose at home!

COACH

Damn right! Go on, hit the showers and have a good weekend! It was a
tough game alright, and Tuesday's going to be a lotta fun. For me anyway!
(laughs)

KEN

I can guess what that bloody means.

BILL

My back is so sore, it's like a truck run over me or something.

COACH

Don't hit the grog too hard boys. We need 110% next week!

EVERYONE

Yeah, yeah!

*The camera pans the disconsolate faces of the players as
they shower, and change.*

---

76. EXT. CLUB ROOMS   **MOMENTS LATER**

*Rose is waiting for Jimmy to come out of the change rooms
as Ken and Bill waltz by her.*

BILL

Hi Rose.

ROSE

Hi Bill, Ken.

BILL

Not our best game eh?

ROSE

It was only one game. I'm not panicking just yet.

KEN

Thanks Rose, yeah, Jimmy won't be long
(catching sight of Jimmy)
Here he is! See yous all later.

ROSE, BILL & JIMMY

Yeah, see you!

Bill and Ken disappear down the laneway and Rose and Jimmy kiss tenderly. From a distance we see Rose having an earnest chat with Jimmy. He looks quite excited. They walk out hand in hand. We see a shot of gran looking very troubled as she makes her way home with a few friends.

---

77. INT ITALIAN RESTAURANT   **LATER**

ROSE

I thought it would be a good surprise for you, and all.

JIMMY

Yeah! Don't ya want to live here when we're married though?

ROSE

To be honest, no! I really want to get away from here. I love Gran and all, but I can't make a move without everyone giving me some direction or advice. I'm sort of drowning in it. Do you know what I mean?

JIMMY

Sort of. But Gran is going to be mighty upset with us!

ROSE

I know.

As they are talking, the manager of the restaurant waltzes over with a bottle and three glasses, and plonks himself down, uninvited, at their table. Jimmy is a bit annoyed and just winks at Rose.

JIMMY

Sorry love, ya know what he's like. G'day mate!

RESTAURANTEUR

Wasn't your best game today mate! What happened to you then?

JIMMY

Oh ya know, my head was elsewhere
(smiling at Rose)
but I'm focused now mate. Last game next week before the finals, so I'll be back! Don't yous worry!

RESTAURANTEUR
(opening the bottle and pouring some red wine)
You better! I'm your biggest fan!

JIMMY
Yeah yeah!

The scene dissolves as they all banter superficially and toast each other's good fortune, with Jimmy and Rose sharing the odd look of resignation.

78. INT KEN'S PLACE   SAME NIGHT

Ken is cooking for Rita and they are having a chat over the stove in the kitchen area.

RITA
I was thinking that we should buy Jimmy and Rose a nice present for their wedding. What do you think?

KEN
Yeah, it would be the right thing to do. Any ideas?

RITA
Well I was looking at a fondue set in town a few days back, and the fella told me it was a sure fire winner as a gift. Something different too!

KEN
Yeah! If you think so. I've never even heard of 'em . I bet no-one else will give 'em one.
(laughs)
What is it anyway?

RITA
Well he did tell me, I could bring it back if you didn't like it.

KEN
What, you bought it then did you?

RITA
Yeah, I sort of got carried away. I'll show it to you.
(she goes into another room and comes back beaming with a fancy box)
We can read all about it after dinner if you like?

KEN
Now that sounds like fun!

RITA
(somewhat concerned)
It's OK isn't it Ken?

KEN
Yeah! I was only kidding with you.
(starts serving up the food))
You know Bill told me about this lady in the hospital, used to be a friend of my dad.

RITA

Yeah!

KEN

Yeah! Well I would like to meet her one day and sort of have a chat about the old days. I've never talked about my dad with anyone who really knew him.

RITA

I always reckon that if you are planning to do something, you better do it before something else happens and, you know what I mean?

KEN

Yeah! You're right! I'm going to try to see her this coming week! Bill will set it up for me, don't you reckon?

RITA

I'm sure he will. He's a top guy, and he sure likes you a lot.

KEN

I know.

The scene dissolves with a comfortable scene of Ken and Rita eating, laughing and enjoying each other's company.

---

79. INT GRAN'S HOME   **THAT SAME NIGHT**

Gran is doing some house work alone, there is a radio on in the background, and she is deep in thought as she dusts down some old photos. She seems a little irritated and annoyed, and is not her bubbly self.

---

80. INT COACH'S HOME   **THAT SAME NIGHT**

There a lot of people milling around drinking beer and eating fish and chips. The coach appears very distracted. His wife and kids carry on superficially as do the other guests as they analyse the game that they'd lost a few hours earlier.

COACH

(philosophically)
We needed a loss before the finals.

FRIEND

Yeah yeah! What about next week Frank?

COACH

No. She'll be right. It's bad luck to go into a finals series without a loss. I remember we did that once. And blow me down if we couldn't manage a win once the finals began. It was like we set our sights on getting there. But not actually winning them.

After a while, no-one is actually listening to him anymore and the scene dissolves with beer being spilt on the carpet,.

81.   **INT BILL'S HOUSE**   **THAT SAME NIGHT**

Bill is taking it easy, running a hot bath, and then climbing into it alone. He expresses some real relief as he slides into the tub and just wallows in the steaming hot water as the scene dissolves out.

82.   **INT MONDAY NIGHT**   **BILL'S SCHOOL**

Bill meets up with the principal and two other fellas in the principal's office.

PRINCIPAL

Hi Bill, thanks for staying back.

BILL

That's OK.

PRINCIPAL

Bill, this is Mike Zeisters and Ted Murray.

BILL

G'day!

PRINCIPAL.

(to Bill)

It's about that application for Scotch College that you put in.

TED

I understand you're very keen to teach physics at VCE level?

BILL

That's true! I've really wanted to extend myself beyond Junior School science. I love it here as you know, but my heart is really in the physics department.

PRINCIPAL

I know.
(turning to Mike and Ted)
Bill has even taken on a playing role in our local football team.

MIKE

That is good news! We like to hear things like that, as it improves relationships with parents and of course the whole community.

TED

That's right, Scotch is also very sport minded. It is a big plus.

BILL

(looking confident)
You're serious, aren't you?

MIKE

Bill, I can assure you, that if you're interested, things could happen quite quickly. When we advertised the position, naturally we got a lot of applicants, but yours really sparked our interest. We've spoken to your Principal over the phone at length, and that's it! We want you!

BILL
I don't know what to say.

MIKE
To let us know in a week from now would be alright.

BILL
I couldn't just walk out on my class midterm. Not to mention the footy
finals!

MIKE
Of course not! We would expect you to actually finish the school year here
and then ship out a few days later. If you agree! What do you think?

BILL
(a bit shell shocked)
It is something I always aspired to. You know, I love teaching.

MIKE
Sounds good to me.

BILL
End of the year eh?

*They all nod to each other as another teacher comes in
with a tray of tea and biscuits and the scene fades with
agreeable handshakes all round.*

83.	**INT BILL'S HOME**	**LATER THAT NIGHT**

The phone is ringing as Bill gets in from the school meeting.

BILL
Hello ... Bill Watson here

WARD SISTER
(off screen)
Oh Mr Watson, I'm glad I caught you. We are planning to release Mrs
Robinson tomorrow afternoon and I'm wondering if you could be here to
perhaps take her home and settle her in?

BILL
Of course I can.

WARD SISTER
That's very kind of you.

BILL
That's alright. What time would suit?

WARD SISTER
Oh any time after five would be fine.

BILL
I finish training around six, so if six thirty is OK?

WARD SISTER

Oh yes! That'll be fine, we'll feed her her dinner, and get her ready.

BILL

OK then I'll see you then!

WARD SISTER

See you then.

*Bill hangs up the phone and pours himself a glass of red
wine and sits lost in thought. He also places a huge wad of
papers onto the kitchen table and proceeds to mark them
assiduously as the scene fades out.*

84.   **INT FOOTBALL TRAINING**   **4PM**

*Bill is tying his football boots on as Ken, already in full gear,
glides over and sits next to him.*

KEN

Running late today mate?

BILL

(laughing)
When you get to my age!

KEN

(seriously)
Bill, I wanted you to be the first to know.

BILL

(looking directly at Ken)
What do you mean?

KEN

Rita and I. We're going to do it!

BILL

You're going to get married!

KEN

Yeah! The plan is to get engaged like. Just after the footy season finishes.
Around the time of Jimmy's marriage.

*By this time Jimmy has waltzed in and as he starts to take
off his suit, next to Ken, overhears his news.*

JIMMY

Bloody great news! Congrats Kenny! But I got some news too!

BILL

Yeah! Congrats Ken! That's wonderful news! Looks like we all got good
news to tell eh?

JIMMY

Carlton mate!

KEN

You mean the beer?

JIMMY

Bloody Carlton! The Blues and all that!

BILL

What about them?

JIMMY

They sent me a form to attend pre-season with them, starting in
November! What about that?

KEN

That's sensational Jimmy! Couldn't have happened to a better guy than
you. Are you going to do it?

JIMMY

I dunno! Rose is pushing me hard to, but it's a huge step eh?

BILL

My news is also about change guys.

*They all look very seriously at Bill, and other players start
milling around them .*

BILL (cont'd)

I've been accepted at Scotch College in Melbourne. Starting in December!

JIMMY

Wow! That sure tops my news eh?

KEN

Congrats to you Bill!

BILL

Thanks guys!

KEN

I'll miss you a lot man!

BILL

Me too! By the way Ken, you remember that old lady Poss?

KEN

Yeah!

BILL

Well she's being let out of hospital today and I was sort of wondering if
you'd come with me to take her home and all.

KEN

Sure!

COACH

(bellowing at them all)

I don't care if it is raining cats and dogs, after last week's miserable effort, we got work to do! So shake a leg and git out there!

Montage: All the players scramble to their feet and slap Bill and Jimmy on the back as they go racing out the doors into the pouring rain to do their laps. We see a few scenes of football training with stab passes and handball drill followed by a gruelling series of hundred yard dashes that are broken up by push-ups and sit-ups. Everyone is exhausted by the end of the session.

85. INT/EXT BILL'S CAR   6:30 PM

Bill and Ken are driving and then reaching the hospital grounds.

BILL

You coming?

KEN

(gingerly)

Nah! You bring her out, I'll stay in the car if you don't mind?

They both laugh.

BILL

Suit yourself!

Bill and Ken get out of the car as the rain finally stops, and as Bill goes inside to collect Poss, Ken gets into the back seat and clears some of the papers that are there. When Bill and Poss finally get back, Poss goes to the back seat and sits next to Ken.

KEN

Wouldn't you like to sit in the front?

POSS

(sighing heavily, with tears in her eyes)

You're your father's son all right! I knew I'd recognize you.

KEN

(Also a bit teary)

So you knew my dad did you?

POSS

You could say we spoke the same language and travelled many of the same roads. He was alright your dad, a good man! I never knew he had a son. I always thought I was the last.

KEN

Well, he wasn't the best communicator, with us, I mean. I didn't know him that well myself. But I'd like to get to know him through you if you don't mind?

POSS

Not tonight son! I'm a bit tired tonight. But we can talk. Talk is a good
thing.

BILL

Where to Poss? Is it far from here?

POSS

Oh no! Everything in my life is real close to our land.
(looking at Ken))
You know what I mean?

KEN

Yeah!

POSS

Next street on the right! I live in that block on the third floor. 306!

*They pull into a rundown apartment block, very bleak
colours, and the driveway full of holes that are half filled
with rain water. Ken and Bill look around with slight shock
on their faces. After parking the car, Poss, Ken and Bill, in
silence, scramble up the concrete stairs to the third floor.
Poss lets them in.*

---

86. INT POSS' APARTMENT   **7PM**

---

*Bill, Ken and Poss enter. A bottle of old milk is on the sink.
Bill glares at Ken and wrinkles his nose at the smell. There
is a lot of dust and grime everywhere.*

BILL

(passionately)
We better clean this place up, else you'll be back in that hospital before
you know where you are.

POSS

(a little embarrassed)
Na! Leave it alone! I'll be OK! You've done enough! I'll be OK!

BILL

(already starting to tidy up the mess)
Can't do that Poss, you can't live like this! Sorry!

KEN

(noticing an old dusty photo on the mantelpiece)
That's my dad, isn't it?

POSS

Yeah! We were good friends in the old days, you know.

KEN

No! I didn't know! Like I said, I never knew my dad that much.

BILL

(assessing the situation and taking control)
There's no way we can do this! You can't stay here Poss! Look, come and stay with me at my place, I got another room at the back …

KEN

(forceful and emotionally charged)
No! We are family! Aren't we? You come and live with me and Rita! We'll take care of you.

POSS

Fighting over me are you?

KEN

(Looking very strangely at Bill)
What happens when you leave town, and forget us?

BILL

(looking hurt)
You know me better than that!

KEN

(a little embarrassed)
Sorry Bill! But, what then?

BILL

I could sort something out!

KEN

You mean well Bill, but her and me, we're the last. You know! You brought us together, but it's my privilege to be the one to care for her from now on! OK?

BILL

If you're sure! Is that OK with you Poss?

KEN

(picking up his dad's photo)
I'm taking you home with me!

POSS

(smiling and looking very proudly at Ken)
I'm awful glad you two are friends.

BILL

(putting his arm around Ken)
That we are! I was his teacher for a time. Now, it appears, he's mine!

They all share a look of affection and understanding.

---

87. INT GRAN'S HOUSE   **MORNING**

Gran is seen prettying herself up with make-up and a floral dress. She is constantly looking into the mirror and smiling to herself.
She grabs her bag and rushes out.

Montage: Gran has a strange look on her face as she waits impatiently for her bus to arrive. Some friends of hers walk by and say a casual "hello" and are surprised when she totally ignores them, oblivious of all and sundry.

Her bus comes and she gets on, pays the fare and takes a seat by a window, about halfway in the bus. We can observe the resolute look in her eyes.

After a few minutes, the bus stops outside a big building in a semi industrial part of the town, and she gets off and marches defiantly through the glass door entrance.

The reception desk is very neatly and tastefully decked out with brochures. There is a large clock on the wall showing the time to be eleven thirty. A young blond lady is seen typing a letter and is a little surprised to see someone at the counter.

YOUNG GIRL
(surprised)
Oh I'm sorry! I didn't notice you there.

GRAN
That's alright dear, is Jimmy Rivers in today?

YOUNG GIRL
Yes he is! Who can I say wants him?

GRAN
It's just a family matter.

YOUNG GIRL
OK, I'll give him a call, I'm sure he's in his office.

The young girl dials a number on her switchboard phone and gets through to Jimmy.

YOUNG GIRL (cont'd)
There's a lady here to see you Jimmy if you can come to the front desk.

The young girl puts down the phone and smiles across to Gran.

YOUNG GIRL (cont'd)
He'll be right down, won't you take a seat?

GRAN
(Still standing)
Thank you dear.

Jimmy comes rushing into the reception area with a concerned look on his face. He greets Gran warmly though.

JIMMY RIVERS

(tense)

Hi Gran, there's nothing wrong is there?

GRAN

(reassuringly)

Oh no! Hi Jimmy, how are you?

JIMMY RIVERS

(relieved)

That's good! I thought something must have happened to Rose that's all.
What brings yous down this part of town?

GRAN

I had to see someone not far from here and I thought we might have lunch
together if you've got the time?

JIMMY RIVERS

I'll make time!

Jimmy grabs a counter phone and dials up.

JIMMY RIVERS (cont'd)

Hi Tim, is it OK if I take an early lunch, as my Gran has popped in to the
office.

TIM

(off screen)

What about the construction project we were
(pausing)

No! That'll be OK, just look in on me when you get back, and enjoy your
lunch.

JIMMY RIVERS

Thanks mate! I'll see yous in an hour!

Jimmy smiles over at Gran as he puts the phone down.

JIMMY RIVERS (cont'd)

There's not too many nice places around here, but if yous don't mind a
sandwich at the deli.

GRAN

Sounds alright to me.

JIMMY RIVERS

OK then!

*Gran and Jimmy go outside and make their way down the
street to a little sandwich bar.*

90. INT SANDWICH BAR

*They both go inside and order a sandwich and coffee
which they receive at the counter and then carry it over to
a table. There are not many people in the deli at this time.*

JIMMY RIVERS

This is a mighty nice surprise Gran!

GRAN

Jess! Call me Jess!

JIMMY RIVERS

OK, Jess.

They look at each for a few nervous seconds and then bite into their sandwiches.

GRAN

(nervously but forthright)

I haven't felt this way for such a long time

JIMMY RIVERS

(a little alarmed)

What are yous saying Gran, Jess?

GRAN

You're the one! I always knew Garry would come back for me if he could.

JIMMY RIVERS

(a little confused)

What in the hell are yous on about?

GRAN

I still know how to make a man happy.

JIMMY RIVERS

(getting up from the table and looking incredulously at Gran)

Are yous nuts! I'm marrying your grand-daughter, not you!

GRAN

(still quietly sitting)

She'll never make you as happy as I can!

By this time, a few people have entered the deli, and, on recognising Jimmy, have focussed their attention to him and his discussion. Jimmy is getting very embarrassed as he makes his way alone to the door.

JIMMY RIVERS

(nervously)

I'll see yous later!

Jimmy rushes through the door and in a flash is gone from view. Gran ignores the strange looks she is getting from all around, and quietly finishes her sandwich and coffee.

---

91. INT GRAN'S   **FRIDAY 7PM**

Jimmy, Rose, Gran and the two brothers of Rose have just finished a roast dinner and are talking table talk while waiting for dessert and coffee. Gran is not talking and is looking quite dejected and sad.

ROSE

(concerned)
Anything wrong Gran?

GRAN

(looking hurt)
I know it's not my business! But Rose, it's like you've turned away from me
all of a sudden!

ROSE

(looking miffed)
Oh come on Gran!

GRAN

What have I ever done to you and your brothers? Tell me that?

ROSE

Nothing Gran! You were the best!

GRAN

So why are you taking him away from me? Tell me that? Why are you doing
that to me?

ROSE

(becoming more assertive)
I'm not prepared to share Jimmy like that! With any other woman! Even
though I'll always love you to bits, you got to understand and to let go! You
got to give me my chance with the man I love!

*Everyone is stunned into a silence that is so out of left field
to shock. Jimmy goes up to Rose and puts his arms around
her, but she shrugs him off, as she goes over to Gran and
hugs her with tears streaming down both their faces.*

ROSE

You got to understand me Gran! He's not Garry! You got to let go of him
before we all get beyond where we can recover from!

JIMMY RIVERS

(concerned)
I know I went through a time where some weird things were happening
to me. But those thoughts and feelings are only a distant memory, like
a dream, and I'm sorry I said anything. I never meant it to hurt anyone!
Honest! Least of all, all of yous here. You're my family now!

GRAN

(resignedly)
Rose's right I guess. Ever since you told us that story! I'm sorry Rose.

JIMMY RIVERS

(trying to lighten up the mood)
Anyway I haven't made the team yet! It's not a given that I will too! Based
on last week's performance!

GRAN

Oh you'll make the team alright son. If it's one thing I know. I know my footy! They'll be clambering to get their hands on you once you start doing your stuff! Garry would have been mighty proud of you, you know.

ROSE

Oh Gran, I love you!

GRAN

I know you do, and I love all of you too.

The scene dissolves straight into the Saturday football match.

---

92. EXT FOOTBALL GROUND   **3PM**

Jimmy, Bill, Ken and Wally (from the other team) are all shining in the wet conditions. Jimmy has just kicked a goal and the crowd has jumped to its feet yelling his name and clapping.

BILL

(running over from the backline to congratulate Jimmy)

That's the stuff! You're back! We don't lose here today do we!

JIMMY RIVERS

(relieved)

Thanks mate! Bloody beauty!

Montage: Scenes of football action and of Gran and Rose sitting happily together cheering with the crowd.

The home team wins well as there is a shot of the scoreboard.   Everyone is ecstatic and buzzing when the team finally comes off the ground and is spoken to by the coach in the change rooms.

---

93. INT. CLUB ROOMS   **MOMENTS LATER**

COACH

(all smiles but deeply serious)

That was great guys! I mean it! You did yourselves and me proud today!
(a lot of cheering)

But the job's not done yet. I've seen plenty of teams set their sights on getting to the finals only to be knocked out once they got there.
(deathly silence all of a sudden)

They made the mistake of aiming too low! I want you to start thinking, all of you, not only to get into that damn grand final! But to bloody win it!
(a lot of cheering)

Nice game Jimmy, Steve, Ken! Go on and enjoy the moment and I'll see you on Tuesday! Well done guys!
(a lot of cheering)

The scene fades out on happy faces hugging and yelling as they drink some Cokes and munch oranges.

Montage: We see a montage of the week in bits and pieces of everyone's lives. Ken with Poss and Rita cohabiting nicely together. Jimmy on the job in his office. Bill in his school routine. There are also scenes of people watching the team train on the Tuesday and Thursday. The regular Friday night meal at Gran's. All the scenes seem a little surreal only to come back to earth on the Saturday of the first finals match.

95. INT CITY FOOTBALL GROUND   **2PM**

MAC

(jokingly with his hands in prayer)
Jimmy, Please kick a bag today! I'm begging!

JIMMY RIVERS

(kidding around)
I'm the one that's begging!

COACH

(watching from a distance)
Cut it out you two! Just make sure you're not the one to let the team down today!
(pointing at Mac)
Make sure it's not you, son!

MAC

(very confidently)
It won't be me coach! It won't be any of us! Will it boys?

Everyone starts yelling and Ken goes over to Bill and quietly chats to him.

KEN

(uiet and serious)
I'm sorry what I said last week when we picked up Poss, it was ....

BILL

It's OK. I understand.

KEN

You might think you do. But believe me, I've faced plenty in my time, and I got confused and upset over seeing my dad's photo. You're the best friend I've got in this town! I just wanted you to know that's all.

BILL

I'm glad you told me that. You're special Ken, and I'm mighty proud to call you my friend.

They both embrace and share the moment, while the changing room keeps getting louder and louder. Pretty soon the coach quietens them down.

COACH
Shut up guys! Shut up! I can't hear myself fart!

Everyone suddenly stops and looks at the coach.

COACH (cont'd)
Plenty of time for that, after the game!
(looking around the room at them all)
You can win today if you follow the principles of the game. We've been doing it all season! So don't forget the things we've trained for! I also want you to protect your team-mates at all costs! Last time we played this mob I noticed a few times where they would knock one of our players down and we just didn't say anything. That was good control, but today, I want you to show some emotion out there and let them know … we are a team that looks after our own!
(a lot of cheering)
Go on! Do us all proud!

96. EXT FOOTBALL GROUND   MOMENTS LATER

MONTAGE: The team jogs out onto the oval to the wild applause of the fans, and we see familiar faces in the crowd like Rose and Gran, Rita and Poss.

A montage of football to show the game with the team winning quite comfortably. Many shots focus on Jimmy and Bill who have been the stars.

97. INT CHANGE ROOMS

COACH
(Excited but in control as he pats each player on the back as they come back into the changing room)
Great game! Great game! Top game Bill! Great game!
(a lot of cheering)
There's one game to go boys, and I know there's a lot of pressure around, because of what it means for this club, after being down on the bottom for so long, to really stick it right up 'em!
(a lot of cheering)
So with a week's break it will be a light session this coming week with a few skill drills!
(a lot of cheering)
Well done today, but the job's not done yet!
(a lot of cheering)

The scene fades out on the packed changing room with fans and players milling around. We see a nice shot of Jimmy and Rose in an embrace.

98. THE SCENE RESUMES WITH A HEADER "TWO WEEKS LATER"

The players are preparing for their Grand Final. It is unusually quiet and tense in the change rooms and the coach addresses the team before they go onto the field.

COACH (cont'd)
(serious and tense)
You guys did everything that's been asked of you this season. And we didn't have everything our own way either at times. Today, well it's about doing for yourselves! Something to look back on when the body's gone,
(pats his stomach)
and the smell of liniment is just a faint memory! I want you to remember this moment! As a marker in time so to speak! So let's all link arms and do this one!
(a lot of cheering))
You've earned it! So now go out and win it!
(a lot of cheering)

The teams jogs out on to the field to the roar of the spectators with footballs to kick into the crowd.

99. EXT ON THE GROUND   2:30

At a given signal, some of the players run towards the boundary line and kick their footballs into the outer crowds, while others actually hand their footballs to the kids that are thronging on the boundary. To the roar of the crowd, Jimmy sets fly with a monster kick that splits the centre of the goals and careers off to be marked by a happy fan. Suddenly the match ball in the centre gets bounced and the game is on.

Ken is the first to see the ball running free, and like in that early training session, he races after it with two opponents hot on his heels. In a delicate manoeuvre Ken handballs to Mac who quickly handballs back to Ken. Ken runs in and kicks a goal, the first score of the game. Everyone is wild with enthusiasm.

KEN
(smiling to Mac)
Thanks Mac!

They embrace

MAC
(jubilant)
Great play mate! Let's do it again eh?

KEN
That's just what I had in mind!

They both laugh to each other!

The first quarter action sees the team scoring the first five goals before the opposition starts a revival. Shots of main scoreboard at quarter time showing the score 5:2 to 2:3.

COACH

(tense)

Steve, you got to expect that they are going to go straight down the middle! Stay with your man, son! You're letting him roam too much!

STEVE

(embarrassed)

Sorry coach, I'll try harder.

COACH

(looking at everyone now)

It's always going to be a tough game, but be responsible for your man! Feed Jimmy!

The siren sounds.

COACH (cont'd)

Go on give it to 'em!

Much cheering erupts from the crowd.

Both teams run to their respective positions and we see a lot of montage shots of action. The score at half time is 8:5 to 6:6 and the players look quite exhausted as they run into the change room for the break.

100. INT CHANGE ROOMS

BILL

(to Jimmy)

That resting ruckman is only there to stop you! I reckon you got to start leading further up the ground and run him out of position a bit. It might put the pressure back on them. What do you think?

JIMMY RIVERS

(concerned)

What about the coach?

BILL

Trust me, it'll work! Give it a go!

JIMMY RIVERS

OK! But it better!

101. EXT FOOTBALL GROUND

In the third quarter, Jimmy, to the amazement of the coach, starts to leave the goal square time and time again, running the full back and the resting ruckman into "no man's land". The result is that Ken begins to play as a loose man in attack, and by the end of the third term has kicked four goals that quarter from that play. The three quarter time scores are then 14:8 to 8:8.

COACH

(hopping mad to Jimmy)

What are you doing son! You're there to kick goals, not prance around the fucking centre!

JIMMY RIVERS

It worked though! Didn't it?

COACH

Yeah! It did then! But it won't in the last quarter, I'll bet my balls on it, and yours! Go back to the square, please!

JIMMY RIVERS

OK!

COACH

Let's get this job done! We're so close! Kick to Jimmy, let him get a couple more goals and we'll breeze this OK?

(a lot of cheering)

JIMMY RIVERS

(quietly to Bill)

Yous were right mate! That was some move eh?

BILL

(serious)

They weren't expecting it mate, it won't work so well this quarter. So do what the coach said and lead into the dead pocket, close to the goals, you'll be OK.

JIMMY RIVERS

(running back into his position with Bill)

You're the man!

Montage: more football action with Jimmy kicking a couple of goals and Ken getting one from a handball from Mac right in the square, seconds before the siren rings out. The team having won the premiership by forty points. Mac and Ken embrace in a bear hug as pandemonium breaks out all over the ground. We see Gran and Rose hugging and crying. The coach rushing over to all of his players with genuine emotion. Ken going over to Bill.

BILL

(wiping tears from his eyes)

You did it Ken! What a game!

KEN

(Also emotional)

We did it Bill! I can't believe it! We did it!

BILL

Your six goals mate! That's what we won by!

KEN

That's the most I've ever got in a game eh?

BILL
(proudly)
You sure saved your best for the biggest game alright! If you're not "best on ground" I'll go hee!

One of the trainers races over to Bill and Ken - smiles all round.

TRAINER
(very excited)
You guys! You were wonderful! Especially you Kenny! Bloody beauty!

KEN
Thanks mate! Wow!

TRAINER
(seriously to Ken)
You know, I've finally worked it out! Who you remind me of.

KEN
(interestedly)
Yeah? Who'd that be then?

TRAINER
Oh a fella called Snowy.

KEN
Oh yeah! Who's he?

TRAINER
Oh he played with us a long time back, that's all.

KEN
Thanks for telling me!

By this time everyone is crowding around where Ken is and the coach whispers in Ken's ear mighty proudly.

COACH
You've won the bloody "Anderson Medal" son! Well done!

KEN
What's that coach?

COACH
(louder so everyone else hears)
Best on bloody ground!

KEN
(taken aback)
Really? Wow! But we won the premiership didn't we? It's like a dream!

JIMMY RIVERS
(proudly)
Yeah mate! We all won it! Everyone of us! Yeah!

Montage: Gran and Rose make their way down the stand to where the players are and hug them all. Rita sits quietly in another stand with Poss waving madly for Ken. He finally sees them and waves back. We see the restaurateur yelling madly and running towards Jimmy. The headmaster of the school has a wry grin on his face as he takes in the scene before him. Young Wally, dressed in jeans and a smartly coloured shirt, goes down and congratulates Ken and Bill. It is a magical moment as the shot dissolves and we see the proud faces of the past players looking extra proud at the old ground.

The new dissolve takes us back to the ground and we see in the mix of people leaving the ground, Ken's boss with a huge grin on her face.

102. INT CITY HOTEL 7PM

It is packed as we see the team, all dressed in suits and led by their coach, come in together in a very surreal atmosphere. All of the guests stand and applaud them.

MC
(proudly)
Has this been a great year or what?
(wild yelling and clapping)
We don't win too many of these flags, so before we read out the last of the "fairest and best" votes, I've arranged a little treat of about two minutes worth! Scotty could you turn the lights off and switch the machine on? It's the only footage we've got from our last flag in 1947! So here it is!

The crowd goes silent as the scratchy film is played. In the film we see an Aboriginal player race after the ball and kick a goal, and the room is filled with cheering.

MC (cont'd)
It isn't much, but our history was built on days like that, and this! Anyway the votes for today's game are 1 vote to Mac Evans, 2 votes to Bruce Wright and 3 votes to Ken Merryman! Bloody great game son!
(a lot of cheering)
The winner, by a country mile, is Jimmy Rivers with 45 points from Ken Merryman with 38 points! Come on up Jimmy!

A lot of cheering, as Jimmy makes his way to the stand and accepts the trophy.

JIMMY
(humbly)
Thanks John. Thanks coach for giving us a go, and thanks guys for passing the ball to me!
(everyone laughs!)
(a lot of cheering)
This has been the best year of my life in so many ways and I'll never forget yous all! Never!

Jimmy locks eyes with Alan Tomlinson. There is a lot of general cheering.

JIMMY (cont'd)

Bad luck Kenny, but you'll be up here next year! That's my prediction! Yous had a great season as well!

A lot more cheering, and Jimmy leaves the stand with Rose at his side. We see a shot of the old trainer getting close to Ken and chatting to him.

TRAINER

(proudly)
Did you see Snowy?

KEN

(looking around the room)
No! Where is he?

TRAINER

Oh, I meant in the old film! That was him kicking that goal!

KEN

Oh yeah! That was him was it?

TRAINER

(proudly)
Yeah! He played over two hundred games with us! A real champion he was!

KEN

So what happened to him then?

TRAINER

Oh he's dead now! But his wife, she stayed on to mind the old ground you know. Had a stroke I believe about a year back. Don't know where she is now, though I would have heard if she'd died or something.

KEN

(looking shocked)
You aren't talking about Poss are you?

TRAINER

Yeah! That's her name! You know her do you?

KEN

(quietly)
Oh yeah! I'm getting to!

TRAINER

This club has got a lot of stories like that! We got a long history! Remind me some time and I'll tell you a few of 'em!

KEN

(deep in thought)
I'd like that.

As the credits roll, the camera pans the room focusing on all the now familiar faces.

103. CLUB ROOM - CREDITS STILL ROLLING

Camera pans around club rooms as the last rays of the sun stream through the window, highlighting the old photos of the past players.

THE END